ALEXANDER POPE

The Poetry
of Pope

a selection

D1417093

Crofts Classics

GENERAL EDITORS

Samuel H. Beer, *Harvard University*

O. B. Hardison, Jr., *The Folger Shakespeare Library*

John Simon

AHM PUBLISHING CORPORATION
Northbrook, Illinois 60062

On the cover is reproduced an engraving after William Hogarth (1697-1764), entitled "Characters who frequented Button's Coffee-house about the year 1720." Pope is standing on the left. Beside him is Dr. John Arbuthnot, the writer and physician to whom Pope wrote his famous *Epistle*.

Research for cover art by Nigel Foxell.

ISBN: 0-88295-067-3

(Formerly 390-23267-X)

Library of Congress Card Number: 54-5547

PRINTED IN THE UNITED STATES OF AMERICA

733

TWENTIETH PRINTING

CONTENTS

INTRODUCTION

CRITICS have been reluctant to take Pope on his own terms, praising or blaming him mainly because he is like, or not like, other writers who are assumed to be the standards of true poetry. Even in the vigorous Pope revival of the last generation, the common practice was to revise the low estimate of the nineteenth century by showing that, under the deceptive neoclassic surface, Pope shared poetic qualities with Wordsworth and Keats, or (according to a later orthodoxy) with John Donne. Now, perhaps, we are beginning to recognize that Pope is a major poet, not because he anticipates romantic or echoes metaphysical traits —as, to some extent, he undoubtedly does—but because his poems are superlative in their own way. There is no substitute for Pope in our literary inheritance. Since most of us, however, have formed our critical principles and sensibilities on quite different poetic models, we must learn to adapt them to the attributes of Pope's special enterprise.

Like many writers of the neoclassic age, Pope chose to pursue his art under extraordinarily narrow conditions. Typical was his election, for all but a handful of his poems, of the ten-syllable closed couplet—a form permitting little deviation from iambic rhythm, in which most of the paired lines compose some sort of syntactic unit and are marked off further by the weight and finality of the rhyme. The result is that two lines in Pope often function as a stanza does in other poets. For this tight prosody Pope cheerfully surrendered the freedom of the numberless metric and stanzaic patterns left him by his predecessors.

The exigencies of the heroic couplet, which forced many of Pope's contemporaries and successors into evasive maneuvers, second-hand effects, or a comfortable surrender to monotony, stimulated Pope to brilliant discoveries of the possibilities of his medium. To cite one example: his frequent use of a strong medial cesura, or pause, was a way of breaking the lines into smaller units in order to maximize the internal relations among the rhetorical and sonantal parts—relations of parallelism, repetition with variation, contrast, or antithesis, and between couplet and couplet, line and line, half-line and half-line. Take his comment on superannuated coquettes, veterans of the war between the sexes:

> See how the world its veterans rewards!
> A youth of frolics, an old age of cards:
> Fair to no purpose, artful to no end,
> Young without lovers, old without a friend;
> A fop their passion, but their prize a sot;
> Alive, ridiculous, and dead, forgot!

The structure of the lines has been kept deliberately uniform, as foil to an interplay of effects which would have been buried in a freer measure. Notice, for example, the inversions in the initial feet, and the variable stresses after the cesura; the symmetry and alteration in the position of adjectives and nouns; the delightful and unexpected equivalence in sound and sense, as well as grammatical function, between "fop" and "sot." Even the diversification in word length, in Pope's verse, is often highly functional. Placed where it is, the polysyllabic "ridiculous" of the last line is a supple, whip-like epithet, which cracks in the final word, "forgot!" In other passages and for other effects, moreover, Pope will be found to depart from this balanced and antithetic structure in many and most varied ways. We need to read Pope's measures with a prepared ear, and slowly enough to give their complex and subtle qualities a chance to unfold—the manipulation of sound, pause, pace, and figure to suit different matters and ends; the unobtrusive devices for merging couplets into larger narrative, descriptive, or deliberative units, and for articulating these into gracefully ordered wholes; and the almost unfailing ease with which the seemingly rigid medium is molded to the divers cadences of the colloquial voice. Even today, the sensitive reader of Pope gets an insight into the grounds for Dr. Johnson's startling judgment: "To attempt any further improvement in versification will be dangerous. Art and diligence have now done their best. . . ."

As in prosody, so in subject, genre, structure, and diction, Pope pursued a strategy of limitation, converting strict and complex conventions into the positive elements of his poetic achievement, and adapting tested means to the achievement of deliberate and restricted aims. Though he experimented with an epic, he published only mock-epics. The most sustained and taxing endeavor of his hard-working literary life was a translation of Homer. One of his longest original poems, the *Essay on Man,* was a verse-treatise; and of his formal satires and epistles, those which were not specific "imitations" of Horace's poems were all in the general manner of Horace. In these, as in pastoral and such shorter kinds as elegy, eulogy, epitaph, and epigram, Pope's preference was for trials in admittedly minor genres, in which the form was modeled on established precedent, and in which even the style often echoed the felicities of his great predecessors.

By working with so many of the artistic conditions given, Pope might be said to have played it safe. As Dr. Johnson tactfully put it, "He excelled every other writer in poetical prudence: he wrote in such a manner as might expose him to few hazards." But Dr. Johnson also pointed to another side of the matter which is easily overlooked. Pope, he said, has demonstrated "invention," "imagination," and "genius": "a mind active, ambitious, and adventurous, always investigating, always aspiring . . . always endeavoring more than it can do." It is a measure of Pope's invention that, in spite of the restricted artistic possibilities open to him, he never falls into mediocrity or self-repetition. The range is great between the high-spirited *A Farewell to London,* the rallying yet affectionate *Epistle to Martha Blount,* and the dignified eloquence, disguising a highly complex rhetorical scheme, of the panegyric *To Robert Earl of Oxford.* No two of his formal satires —no two even of his great satiric portraits—turn out to be quite alike, in organizing principle, detail of execution, or prevailing tone. Both the *Rape of the Lock* and *The Dunciad* are "heroi-comical," have a well-defined lineage reaching from classic times through Dryden, and apply similar epic episodes and devices to the contemporary scene; but could there be a wider disparity than that between the glitter, beauty, and playfulness of the first, and the murky light and grotesque ponderosity of the second?

Pope's greatest achievements are in satire, and against him it has frequently been argued that since poetry is passion, and satire is intellectual, Pope wrote prose; also (and inconsistently) that while poetry must be noble, satire expresses the mean emotions of malice and hate. It might be replied that for purposes of poetry—to bend the words of Robert Frost to this application—hate

> Is also great
> And would suffice.

But in fact Pope exhibits an astonishing range of feeling in his satires, as the *Epistle to Dr. Arbuthnot* will demonstrate, or on a smaller scale his Moral Essay *On the Characters of Women*, with its flexible transition from the raillery of the beginning, to the severity of the arraignment of Atossa, to the gallantry of the conclusion, where the poet manages the feat of expressing admiration and tenderness for Martha Blount without withdrawing the impeachment attendant upon her being, after all, a woman. Discussions of Pope's waspishness and venom have turned on the question of whether his handling of contemporaries was justifiable by the facts. Recent researches show Pope to have been far more amiable and admirable than people used to think; but this, after all, is a question relevant to his life, and not to his art. Within the province of his satires, Pope is consistently a moralist. In them he assumes and sustains remarkably the position of the magnanimous man, whose natural kindliness is tempered by a stern sense of justice, and whose hate, as he says, is merely "the strong antipathy of good to bad," whether in morals, manners, or intellect. As delineated in his writings, furthermore, living individuals become representative. Whatever Addison himself was like, "Atticus" certainly exists, and deserves what he gets. And whatever Pope was in person, his poetic character is for the most part unimpugnable.

Pope's most characteristic device, finally, was to apply the standards of heroic literature and high tragedy to the trivial follies and vices of his own polite age. He does not, however, ridicule men because they are trivial, but because they remain trivial while capable of greatness. His mock-heroic method sets what man has been, and can be, against what he too often is. And within the realm of burlesque, Pope is entirely capable of rising to grandeur of conception and style. In the great conclusion to *The Dunciad*, the sense of the ludicrous is almost lost in the sublimity and the terror. The passage brings out the sustaining principle underlying all of the poem, and Pope's general philosophy as well. This is the noble neoclassic conception that the excellence of a work of art, the temperament of a wise and good man, and the structure of a society are alike a matter of harmony, proportion, and of order. The order has been hard-won from chaos, through a process analogous to that by which God formed the universe from the confusion of warring atoms. To make a good heroic couplet, therefore, is to shape a bit of chaos into cosmos; while any instance of ineptness in poetry or pedantry in intellect shakes the precarious fabric of civilization. What Pope presents, then, in this passage written almost at the end of his life, is an apocalyptic vision of the triumph of the massed forces of Dullness, which would involve the return of all order to the primeval anarchy:

> Lo! thy dread empire, Chaos! is restored;
> Light dies before thy uncreating word. . . .

Pope's art is neoclassic, in that it is a triumph of grace and seeming freedom within drastically regulated and traditional patterns. At its best it also meets the test of all great poetry, for its potentialities are such as to yield new discoveries at each reading. To the question, already old in his day, "Is Pope a poet?" Hazlitt long ago made the pertinent rejoinder: "And shall we cut ourselves off from beauties like these with a theory?"

The basis for the text of most of the poems is the edition which William Warburton, Pope's executor, published in 1751. Several of the poems I have included were not published until a later date, and in the instance of some others, I have gone back to the readings in an earlier edition than Warburton's. When this would not affect the rhyme, I have modernized the spellings and filled in elided letters, and I have occasionally altered the punctuation where older conventions might mislead a modern reader. The date at the end of each item is that of first publication; if there is a second date, it indicates Pope's publication of a radical revision of his original attempt. Notes have been added when they seemed sufficiently advantageous to be worth the displacement of Pope's own text. All poems (including Book iv of *The Dunciad*, originally published as a separate piece) are reproduced in their entirety. And to indicate the scope of Pope's achievement, I have included several of his shorter poems which deserve to be better known than they are.

PRINCIPAL DATES IN POPE'S LIFE

1688   Alexander Pope born in London, May 21, of Roman Catholic parents. His father a retired merchant, moderately well-to-do. [The Great Revolution].

c. 1700   Pope's family moved to Binfield, in Windsor Forest. [Death of Dryden].

1705   Began acquaintance with literary men in London, including Wycherley, Congreve, and the gentleman-critic, William Walsh, who encouraged and advised Pope in his early writing.

1709   The *Pastorals,* his first published work. [Birth of Johnson].

1711   *An Essay on Criticism:* praised by Addison, attacked by John Dennis.

1712   The *Messiah: A Sacred Eclogue; The Rape of the Lock,* first version in two cantos.

1713   *Windsor Forest,* a loco-descriptive poem. Pope a member of the Scriblerus Club, composed of Tory wits including Swift, Arbuthnot, Gay, and Parnell.

1714   *The Rape of the Lock,* expanded version in five cantos. [Death of Queen Anne]. Fall of Tory ministry, and dispersal of Scriblerus writers.

1715   The first volume of Pope's *Iliad.* This translation, Pope's major task until its completion in 1720, earned him fame and a small fortune.

1716   Pope's family moved to Chiswick, near London.

1717   *Verses to the Memory of an Unfortunate Lady* and *Eloisa to Abelard,* published in the first collected volume of Pope's *Works.* Pope's father died.

1718   Pope and his mother moved to Twickenham, his celebrated villa on the Thames, near Richmond.

Pope became a recognized expert in landscape gardening.

1719 [Death of Addison].

1725 Pope's edition of *Shakespeare;* its shortcomings attacked in Lewis Theobald's *Shakespeare Restored* (1726). Pope published vols. i-iii of Homer's *Odyssey*—another highly profitable translation, completed in 1726.

1728 *The Dunciad,* in three books, with Theobald the hero. Reissued, with extensive mock-critical apparatus, as *The Dunciad Variorum* (1729). Beginning of Pope's great career as a verse satirist.

1731 *Epistle to Burlington* (Moral Essay iv); the other *Epistles* (Moral Essays i-iii) were published 1733-35.

1733 Pope's first *Imitation of Horace* (Satire ii, i); the other *Imitations* were published 1734-38. *An Essay on Man,* Epistles i-iii, published anonymously; Epistle iv appeared in 1734.

1735 *Epistle to Dr. Arbuthnot.* [Death of Arbuthnot].

1738 *Epilogue to the Satires,* Pope's last verse satire, a savage denunciation of the political corruption under Sir Robert Walpole.

1740 Meeting and friendship with Warburton, who became Pope's editor and literary executor.

1742 *The New Dunciad* (the fourth book). The complete *Dunciad* in four books was published in 1743, with Colley Cibber the hero.

1744 Pope died, May 30.

Ode on Solitude

HAPPY the man, whose wish and care
  A few paternal acres bound,
Content to breathe his native air,
          In his own ground.

Whose herds with milk, whose fields with bread,
  Whose flocks supply him with attire,
Whose trees in summer yield him shade,
          In winter fire.

Blest, who can unconcernedly find
  Hours, days, and years slide soft away,   10
In health of body, peace of mind,
          Quiet by day,

Sound sleep by night; study and ease,
  Together mixed; sweet recreation;
And innocence, which most does please
          With meditation.

Thus let me live, unseen, unknown,
  Thus unlamented let me die,
Steal from the world, and not a stone
          Tell where I lie.   20

1717-1736

Ode on Solitude said by Pope to have been written before he
was twelve years old, but considerably revised before publica-
tion

The Universal Prayer

Deo Opt. Max.

FATHER of all! in every age,
　In every clime adored,
By saint, by savage, and by sage,
　Jehovah, Jove, or Lord!

Thou great First Cause, least understood:
　Who all my sense confined
To know but this, that Thou art good,
　And that myself am blind;

Yet gave me, in this dark estate,
　To see the good from ill;　　　　　　　　　　10
And binding nature fast in fate,
　Left free the human will.

What conscience dictates to be done,
　Or warns me not to do,
This, teach me more than hell to shun,
　That, more than heaven pursue.

What blessings Thy free bounty gives,
　Let me not cast away;
For God is paid when man receives,
　T' enjoy is to obey.　　　　　　　　　　　20

Yet not to earth's contracted span
　Thy goodness let me bound,
Or think Thee Lord alone of man,
　When thousand worlds are round:

Let not this weak, unknowing hand
　Presume Thy bolts to throw,
And deal damnation round the land
　On each I judge Thy foe.

If I am right, Thy grace impart,
　Still in the right to stay;　　　　　　　　　30
If I am wrong, oh teach my heart
　To find that better way.

Save me alike from foolish pride,
　Or impious discontent,

At aught Thy wisdom has denied,
  Or aught Thy goodness lent.

Teach me to feel another's woe,
  To hide the fault I see;
That mercy I to others show
  That mercy show to me. 40

Mean though I am, not wholly so
  Since quickened by Thy breath;
Oh lead me wheresoe'er I go,
  Through this day's life or death.

This day, be bread and peace my lot:
  All else beneath the sun,
Thou knowst if best bestowed or not,
  And let Thy will be done.

To Thee, whose temple is all space,
  Whose altar, earth, sea, skies! 50
One chorus let all Being raise!
  All Nature's incense rise!

1738

A Farewell to London

IN THE YEAR 1715

DEAR, damned, distracting town, farewell!
  Thy fools no more I'll tease:
This year in peace, ye critics dwell,
  Ye harlots, sleep at ease!

Soft B——s and rough C——s adieu,
  Earl Warwick make your moan,
The lively H——k and you
  May knock up whores alone.

To drink and droll be Rowe allowed
  Till the third watchman's toll; 10
Let Jervas gratis paint, and Frowde
  Save threepence and his soul.

5 B——s and C——s Brocas, a poet, and Craggs, a statesman,
Pope's close friends 7 H——k young Viscount Hinchinbroke,
with whom Pope had shared his cakes and ale

Farewell, Arbuthnot's raillery
  On every learnèd sot;
And Garth, the best good Christian he,
  Although he knows it not.

Lintot, farewell! thy bard must go;
  Farewell, unhappy Tonson!
Heaven gives thee for thy loss of Rowe,
  Lean Philips and fat Johnson.   20

Why should I stay? Both parties rage;
  My vixen mistress squalls;
The wits in envious feuds engage:
  And Homer (damn him!) calls.

The love of arts lies cold and dead
  In Halifax's urn;
And not one Muse of all he fed
  Has yet the grace to mourn.

My friends, by turns, my friends confound,
  Betray, and are betrayed: 30
Poor Y——r's sold for fifty pounds,
  And B——ll is a jade.

Why make I friendships with the great,
  When I no favor seek?
Or follow girls, seven hours in eight?
  I used but once a week.

Still idle, with a busy air,
  Deep whimsies to contrive;
The gayest valetudinaire,
  Most thinking rake, alive.   40

Solicitous for others' ends,
  Though fond of dear repose;
Careless or drowsy with my friends,
  And frolic with my foes.

Luxurious lobster-nights, farewell,
  For sober, studious days!
And Burlington's delicious meal,
  For salads, tarts, and pease!

24 **Homer** whose *Iliad* Pope was then rather painfully engaged
in translating 31-32 **Y**——**r's** and **B**——**ll** Mrs. Younger and
Mrs. Bicknell, actresses

Adieu to all, but Gay alone,
   Whose soul, sincere and free,   50
Loves all mankind, but flatters none,
   And so may starve with me.

1776

Epistle to Martha Blount

ON HER LEAVING THE TOWN AFTER THE CORONATION

As some fond virgin, whom her mother's care
Drags from the town to wholesome country air,
Just when she learns to roll a melting eye,
And hear a spark, yet think no danger nigh;
From the dear man unwilling she must sever,
Yet takes one kiss before she parts forever:
Thus from the world fair Zephalinda flew,
Saw others happy, and with sighs withdrew;
Not that their pleasures caused her discontent,
She sighed not that they stayed, but that she went.   10
   She went, to plain-work and to purling brooks,
Old-fashioned halls, dull aunts, and croaking rooks:
She went from opera, park, assembly, play,
To morning walks, and prayers three hours a day;
To part her time 'twixt reading and bohea,
To muse, and spill her solitary tea,
Or o'er cold coffee trifle with the spoon,
Count the slow clock, and dine exact at noon;
Divert her eyes with pictures in the fire,
Hum half a tune, tell stories to the squire;   20
Up to her godly garret after seven,
There starve and pray, for that's the way to heaven.
   Some squire, perhaps, you take delight to rack,
Whose game is whisk, whose treat a toast in sack;
Who visits with a gun, presents you birds,
Then gives a smacking buss and cries—No words!
Or with his hound comes hallooing from the stable,
Makes love with nods, and knees beneath a table;
Whose laughs are hearty, though his jests are coarse,
And loves you best of all things—but his horse.   30
   In some fair evening, on your elbow laid,
You dream of triumphs in the rural shade;

24 **whisk** old form of "whist"

In pensive thought recall the fancied scene,
See coronations rise on every green;
Before you pass th' imaginary sights
Of lords, and earls, and dukes, and gartered knights,
While the spread fan o'ershades your closing eyes;
Then give one flirt, and all the vision flies.
Thus banish scepters, coronets, and balls,
And leave you in lone woods, or empty walls.   40
  So when your slave, at some dear, idle time,
(Not plagued with headaches, or the want of rhyme)
Stands in the streets, abstracted from the crew,
And while he seems to study, thinks of you;
Just when his fancy points your sprightly eyes,
Or sees the blush of soft Parthenia rise,
Gay pats my shoulder, and you vanish quite,
Streets, chairs, and coxcombs rush upon my sight;
Vexed to be still in town, I knit my brow,
Look sour, and hum a tune — — as you may now.   50

1717

Epigram

ENGRAVED ON THE COLLAR OF A DOG WHICH I GAVE
TO HIS ROYAL HIGHNESS

I AM his Highness' dog at Kew;
Pray tell me, sir, whose dog are you?

1739

To Robert Earl of Oxford and Earl Mortimer

SUCH were the notes thy once-loved poet sung,
Till death untimely stopped his tuneful tongue.

His Royal Highness Frederick Prince of Wales, father of **George III Robert Earl of Oxford** Robert Harley, Earl of Oxford and Mortimer, a member of the Scriblerus Club with Pope, Swift, Parnell, and others. Once head of the Tory Ministry under Queen Anne, he was imprisoned in the Tower from 1715 to 1717, and then retired into the country. This epistle prefaced a posthumous edition of Parnell's *Poems,* which Pope himself published.

Oh just beheld, and lost! admired and mourned!
With softest manners, gentlest arts adorned!
Blest in each science, blest in every strain!
Dear to the Muse! to Harley dear—in vain!

For him, thou oft hast bid the world attend,
Fond to forget the statesman in the friend;
For Swift and him, despised the farce of state,
The sober follies of the wise and great;   10
Dexterous, the craving, fawning crowd to quit,
And pleased to 'scape from flattery to wit.

Absent or dead, still let a friend be dear,
(A sigh the absent claims, the dead a tear)
Recall those nights that closed thy toilsome days,
Still hear thy Parnell in his living lays,
Who, careless now of interest, fame, or fate,
Perhaps forgets that Oxford e'er was great;
Or deeming meanest what we greatest call,
Beholds thee glorious only in thy fall.   20

And sure, if aught below the seats divine
Can touch immortals, 'tis a soul like thine:
A soul supreme, in each hard instance tried,
Above all pain, all passion, and all pride,
The rage of power, the blast of public breath,
The lust of lucre, and the dread of death.

In vain to deserts thy retreat is made;
The Muse attends thee to thy silent shade:
'Tis hers the brave man's latest steps to trace,
Rejudge his acts, and dignify disgrace.   30
When interest calls off all her sneaking train,
And all th' obliged desert, and all the vain;
She waits, or to the scaffold, or the cell,
When the last lingering friend has bid farewell.
Even now, she shades thy evening-walk with bays,
(No hireling she, no prostitute to praise)
Even now, observant of the parting ray,
Eyes the calm sunset of thy various day,
Through fortune's cloud one truly great can see,
Nor fears to tell, that MORTIMER is he.   40

1721

On Receiving from the Right Hon. the Lady Frances Shirley a Standish and Two Pens

YES, I beheld the Athenian queen
    Descend in all her sober charms;
"And take," she said, and smiled serene,
    "Take at this hand celestial arms:

Secure the radiant weapons wield;
    This golden lance shall guard desert,
And if a vice dares keep the field,
    This steel shall stab it to the heart."

Awed, on my bended knees I fell,
    Received the weapons of the sky;   10
And dipped them in the sable well,
    The fount of fame or infamy.

"What well? what weapon?" Flavia cries,
    "A standish, steel and golden pen!
It came from Bertrand's, not the skies;
    I gave it you to write again.

But, friend, take heed whom you attack;
    You'll bring a house (I mean of peers),
Red, blue and green, nay white and black,
    L—— and all about your ears.   20

You'd write as smooth again on glass,
    And run, on ivory, so glib,
As not to stick at fool or ass,
    Nor stop at flattery or fib.

Athenian queen! and sober charms!
    I tell ye, fool, there's nothing in't:
'Tis Venus, Venus, gives these arms;
    In Dryden's Virgil see the print.

Come, if you'll be a quiet soul,
    That dares tell neither truth nor lies,   30
I'll list you in the harmless roll
    Of those that sing of these poor eyes."

1751

Standish a stand for writing materials   **15 Bertrand's** a toy shop
in London   **20 L——** Lambeth, London residence of the Arch-
bishops of Canterbury

EPITAPH

Intended for Sir Isaac Newton

IN WESTMINSTER ABBEY

ISAACUS NEWTONUS:
Quem Immortalem
Testantur Tempus, Natura, Cœlum:
Mortalem
Hoc Marmor Fatetur.

NATURE and Nature's laws lay hid in night:
God said, *Let Newton be!* and all was light.

1730

An Essay on Criticism

PART I

'TIS hard to say, if greater want of skill
Appear in writing or in judging ill;
But, of the two, less dangerous is the offense
To tire our patience, than mislead our sense.
Some few in that, but numbers err in this,
Ten censure wrong, for one who writes amiss;
A fool might once himself alone expose,
Now one in verse makes many more in prose.
　'Tis with our judgments as our watches, none
Go just alike, yet each believes his own.   10
In poets as true genius is but rare,
True taste as seldom is the critic's share;
Both must alike from Heaven derive their light,
These born to judge, as well as those to write.
Let such teach others who themselves excel,
And censure freely who have written well.
Authors are partial to their wit, 'tis true,
But are not critics to their judgment too?
　Yet if we look more closely, we shall find
Most have the seeds of judgment in their mind: 20
Nature affords at least a glimmering light;
The lines, though touched but faintly, are drawn right.

Isaacus Newtonus "Isaac Newton, whom Time, Nature, and the
Heavens proclaim immortal, this marble reveals mortal."

But as the slightest sketch, if justly traced,
Is by ill coloring but the more disgraced,
So by false learning is good sense defaced:
Some are bewildered in the maze of schools,
And some made coxcombs Nature meant but fools.
In search of wit these lose their common sense,
And then turn critics in their own defense:
Each burns alike, who can, or cannot write,   30
Or with a rival's, or an eunuch's spite.
All fools have still an itching to deride,
And fain would be upon the laughing side.
If Maevius scribble in Apollo's spite,
There are who judge still worse than he can write.
   Some have at first for wits, then poets passed,
Turned critics next, and proved plain fools at last.
Some neither can for wits nor critics pass,
As heavy mules are neither horse nor ass.
Those half-learned witlings, numerous in our isle,   40
As half-formed insects on the banks of Nile;
Unfinished things, one knows not what to call,
Their generation's so equivocal:
To tell 'em, would a hundred tongues require,
Or one vain wit's, that might a hundred tire.
   But you who seek to give and merit fame,
And justly bear a critic's noble name,
Be sure yourself and your own reach to know,
How far your genius, taste, and learning go;
Launch not beyond your depth, but be discreet,   50
And mark that point where sense and dullness meet.
   Nature to all things fixed the limits fit,
And wisely curbed proud man's pretending wit.
As on the land while here the ocean gains,
In other parts it leaves wide sandy plains;
Thus in the soul while memory prevails,
The solid power of understanding fails;
Where beams of warm imagination play,
The memory's soft figures melt away.
One science only will one genius fit;   60
So vast is art, so narrow human wit:
Not only bounded to peculiar arts,
But oft in those confined to single parts.
Like kings we lose the conquests gained before,
By vain ambition still to make them more;

34 **Maevius** mediocre poet, contemporary with Virgil

Each might his several province well command,
Would all but stoop to what they understand.
  First follow Nature, and your judgment frame
By her just standard, which is still the same:
Unerring NATURE, still divinely bright,   70
One clear, unchanged, and universal light,
Life, force, and beauty, must to all impart,
At once the source, and end, and test of art.
Art from that fund each just supply provides,
Works without show, and without pomp presides:
In some fair body thus th' informing soul
With spirits feeds, with vigor fills the whole,
Each motion guides, and every nerve sustains;
Itself unseen, but in th' effects remains.
Some, to whom Heaven in wit has been profuse,   80
Want as much more to turn it to its use;
For wit and judgment often are at strife,
Though meant each other's aid, like man and wife.
'Tis more to guide, than spur the Muse's steed;
Restrain his fury, than provoke his speed;
The wingèd courser, like a generous horse,
Shows most true mettle when you check his course.
  Those RULES of old discovered, not devised,
Are Nature still, but Nature methodized:
Nature, like liberty, is but restrained   90
By the same laws which first herself ordained.
  Hear how learned Greece her useful rules indites,
When to repress, and when indulge our flights:
High on Parnassus' top her sons she showed,
And pointed out those arduous paths they trod;
Held from afar, aloft, th' immortal prize,
And urged the rest by equal steps to rise.
Just precepts thus from great examples given,
She drew from them what they derived from Heaven.
The generous critic fanned the poet's fire,   100
And taught the world with reason to admire.
Then criticism the Muse's handmaid proved,
To dress her charms, and make her more beloved:
But following wits from that intention strayed,
Who could not win the mistress, wooed the maid;
Against the poets their own arms they turned,
Sure to hate most the men from whom they learned.
So modern 'pothecaries, taught the art
By doctor's bills to play the doctor's part,
Bold in the practice of mistaken rules,   110

Prescribe, apply, and call their masters fools.
Some on the leaves of ancient authors prey,
Nor time nor moths e'er spoiled so much as they.
Some drily plain, without invention's aid,
Write dull receipts how poems may be made.
These leave the sense, their learning to display,
And those explain the meaning quite away.
   You then whose judgment the right course would steer,
Know well each ancient's proper character;
His fable, subject, scope in every page;   120
Religion, country, genius of his age:
Without all these at once before your eyes,
Cavil you may, but never criticize.
Be Homer's works your study and delight,
Read them by day, and meditate by night;
Thence form your judgment, thence your maxims bring,
And trace the Muses upward to their spring.
Still with itself compared, his text peruse;
And let your comment be the Mantuan Muse.
   When first young Maro in his boundless mind   130
A work t' outlast immortal Rome designed,
Perhaps he seemed above the critic's law,
And but from Nature's fountains scorned to draw:
But when t' examine every part he came,
Nature and Homer were, he found, the same.
Convinced, amazed, he checks the bold design;
And rules as strict his labored work confine,
As if the Stagirite o'erlooked each line.
Learn hence for ancient rules a just esteem;
To copy Nature is to copy them.   140
   Some beauties yet no precepts can declare,
For there's a happiness as well as care.
Music resembles poetry, in each
Are nameless graces which no methods teach,
And which a master-hand alone can reach.
If, where the rules not far enough extend,
(Since rules were made but to promote their end)
Some lucky license answer to the full
Th' intent proposed, that license is a rule.
Thus Pegasus, a nearer way to take,   150
May boldly deviate from the common track;
From vulgar bounds with brave disorder part,
And snatch a grace beyond the reach of art,
Which, without passing through the judgment, gains

129-30 **Mantuan Muse** . . . **Maro** Virgil 138 **Stagirite** Aristotle

The heart, and all its end at once attains.
In prospects thus, some objects please our eyes,
Which out of Nature's common order rise,
The shapeless rock, or hanging precipice.
Great wits sometimes may gloriously offend,
And rise to faults true critics dare not mend.   160
But though the ancients thus their rules invade,
(As kings dispense with laws themselves have made)
Moderns, beware! or if you must offend
Against the precept, ne'er transgress its end;
Let it be seldom, and compelled by need;
And have, at least, their precedent to plead.
The critic else proceeds without remorse,
Seizes your fame, and puts his laws in force.
    I know there are, to whose presumptuous thoughts
Those freer beauties, even in them, seem faults.   170
Some figures monstrous and misshaped appear,
Considered singly, or beheld too near,
Which, but proportioned to their light, or place,
Due distance reconciles to form and grace.
A prudent chief not always must display
His powers in equal ranks, and fair array,
But with th' occasion and the place comply,
Conceal his force, nay seem sometimes to fly.
Those oft are stratagems which errors seem,
Nor is it Homer nods, but we that dream.   180
    Still green with bays each ancient altar stands,
Above the reach of sacrilegious hands;
Secure from flames, from envy's fiercer rage,
Destructive war, and all-involving age.
See from each clime the learned their incense bring!
Hear, in all tongues consenting paeans ring!
In praise so just let every voice be joined,
And fill the general chorus of mankind.
Hail, bards triumphant! born in happier days;
Immortal heirs of universal praise!   190
Whose honors with increase of ages grow,
As streams roll down, enlarging as they flow;
Nations unborn your mighty names shall sound,
And worlds applaud that must not yet be found!
O may some spark of your celestial fire,
The last, the meanest of your sons inspire,
(That on weak wings, from far, pursues your flights;
Glows while he reads, but trembles as he writes)
To teach vain wits a science little known,

T' admire superior sense, and doubt their own!   200

PART II

Of all the causes which conspire to blind
Man's erring judgment, and misguide the mind,
What the weak head with strongest bias rules,
Is PRIDE, the never-failing vice of fools.
Whatever Nature has in worth denied,
She gives in large recruits of needful pride;
For as in bodies, thus in souls, we find
What wants in blood and spirits, swelled with wind:
Pride, where wit fails, steps in to our defense,
And fills up all the mighty void of sense.   210
If once right reason drives that cloud away,
Truth breaks upon us with resistless day.
Trust not yourself; but your defects to know,
Make use of every friend—and every foe.
   A little learning is a dangerous thing;
Drink deep, or taste not the Pierian spring:
There shallow draughts intoxicate the brain,
And drinking largely sobers us again.
Fired at first sight with what the Muse imparts,
In fearless youth we tempt the heights of arts,   220
While from the bounded level of our mind,
Short views we take, nor see the lengths behind;
But more advanced, behold with strange surprise
New distant scenes of endless science rise!
So pleased at first the towering Alps we try,
Mount o'er the vales, and seem to tread the sky,
Th' eternal snows appear already past,
And the first clouds and mountains seem the last:
But, those attained, we tremble to survey
The growing labors of the lengthened way,   230
Th' increasing prospect tires our wandering eyes,
Hills peep o'er hills, and Alps on Alps arise!
   A perfect judge will read each work of wit
With the same spirit that its author writ:
Survey the WHOLE, nor seek slight faults to find
Where Nature moves, and rapture warms the mind;
Nor lose, for that malignant dull delight,
The generous pleasure to be charmed with wit.
But in such lays as neither ebb, nor flow,
Correctly cold, and regularly low,   240
That shunning faults, one quiet tenor keep;

We cannot blame indeed—but we may sleep.
In wit, as Nature, what affects our hearts
Is not th' exactness of peculiar parts;
'Tis not a lip, or eye, we beauty call,
But the joint force and full result of all.
Thus when we view some well-proportioned dome,
(The world's just wonder, and even thine, O Rome!)
No single parts unequally surprise,
All comes united to th' admiring eyes;   250
No monstrous height, or breadth, or length appear;
The whole at once is bold, and regular.

Whoever thinks a faultless piece to see,
Thinks what ne'er was, nor is, nor e'er shall be,
In every work regard the writer's end,
Since none can compass more than they intend;
And if the means be just, the conduct true,
Applause, in spite of trivial faults, is due.
As men of breeding, sometimes men of wit,
T' avoid great errors, must the less commit: 260
Neglect the rules each verbal critic lays,
For not to know some trifles, is a praise.
Most critics, fond of some subservient art,
Still make the whole depend upon a part:
They talk of principles, but notions prize,
And all to one loved folly sacrifice.

Once on a time, La Mancha's knight, they say,
A certain bard encountering on the way,
Discoursed in terms as just, with looks as sage,
As e'er could Dennis, of the Grecian stage;   270
Concluding all were desperate sots and fools,
Who durst depart from Aristotle's rules.
Our author, happy in a judge so nice,
Produced his play, and begged the knight's advice;
Made him observe the subject, and the plot,
The manners, passions, unities; what not?
All which, exact to rule, were brought about,
Were but a combat in the lists left out.
"What! leave the combat out?" exclaims the knight;
Yes, or we must renounce the Stagirite.   280
"Not so, by Heaven" (he answers in a rage)
"Knights, squires, and steeds, must enter on the stage."
So vast a throng the stage can ne'er contain.

267 **La Mancha's knight** Don Quixote, in an episode from Avel-
laneda's spurious *Second Part of Don Quixote* 270 **Dennis** John
Dennis, famous contemporary critic 280 **The Stagirite** Aristotle

"Then build a new, or act it in a plain."
　　Thus critics, of less judgment than caprice,
Curious, not knowing, not exact but nice,
Form short ideas; and offend in arts
(As most in manners) by a love to parts.
　　Some to conceit alone their taste confine,
And glittering thoughts struck out at every line;　　290
Pleased with a work where nothing's just or fit;
One glaring chaos and wild heap of wit.
Poets, like painters, thus, unskilled to trace
The naked Nature and the living grace,
With gold and jewels cover every part,
And hide with ornaments their want of art.
True wit is Nature to advantage dressed;
What oft was thought, but ne'er so well expressed;
Something, whose truth convinced at sight we find,
That gives us back the image of our mind.　　300
As shades more sweetly recommend the light,
So modest plainness sets off sprightly wit.
For works may have more wit than does 'em good,
As bodies perish through excess of blood.
　　Others for language all their care express,
And value books, as women men, for dress:
Their praise is still,—The style is excellent:
The sense, they humbly take upon content.
Words are like leaves; and where they most abound,
Much fruit of sense beneath is rarely found.　　310
False eloquence, like the prismatic glass,
Its gaudy colors spreads on every place;
The face of Nature we no more survey,
All glares alike, without distinction gay:
But true expression, like th' unchanging sun,
Clears, and improves whate'er it shines upon,
It gilds all objects, but it alters none.
Expression is the dress of thought, and still
Appears more decent, as more suitable;
A vile conceit in pompous words expressed,　　320
Is like a clown in regal purple dressed:
For different styles with different subjects sort,
As several garbs, with country, town, and court.
Some by old words to fame have made pretense,
Ancients in phrase, mere moderns in their sense;
Such labored nothings, in so strange a style,
Amaze th' unlearned, and make the learnèd smile.

289 conceit ingenious literary figure or thought

Unlucky, as Fungoso in the play,
These sparks with awkward vanity display
What the fine gentleman wore yesterday;   330
And but so mimic ancient wits at best,
As apes our grandsires, in their doublets dressed.
In words, as fashions, the same rule will hold;
Alike fantastic, if too new, or old:
Be not the first by whom the new are tried,
Nor yet the last to lay the old aside.
  But most by numbers judge a poet's song;
And smooth or rough, with them, is right or wrong:
In the bright muse though thousand charms conspire,
Her voice is all these tuneful fools admire;   340
Who haunt Parnassus but to please their ear,
Not mend their minds; as some to church repair,
Not for the doctrine, but the music there.
These equal syllables alone require,
Though oft the ear the open vowels tire;
While expletives their feeble aid do join;
And ten low words oft creep in one dull line:
While they ring round the same unvaried chimes,
With sure returns of still expected rhymes;
Where'er you find "the cooling western breeze,"   350
In the next line, it "whispers through the trees":
If crystal streams "with pleasing murmurs creep,"
The reader's threatened (not in vain) with "sleep":
Then, at the last and only couplet fraught
With some unmeaning thing they call a thought,
A needless Alexandrine ends the song,
That, like a wounded snake, drags its slow length along.
Leave such to tune their own dull rhymes, and know
What's roundly smooth, or languishingly slow;
And praise the easy vigor of a line,   360
Where Denham's strength, and Waller's sweetness join.
True ease in writing comes from art, not chance,
As those move easiest who have learned to dance.
'Tis not enough no harshness gives offense,
The sound must seem an echo to the sense:
Soft is the strain when Zephyr gently blows,
And the smooth stream in smoother numbers flows;
But when loud surges lash the sounding shore,

328 **Fungoso** a would-be gallant in Ben Jonson's *Every Man Out of His Humour* 356 **Alexandrine** verse-line of six feet 361 **Denham's** . . . **Waller's** seventeenth-century poets often accredited in Pope's time with having "refined" English metrics

The hoarse, rough verse should like the torrent roar:
When Ajax strives some rock's vast weight to throw,   370
The line too labors, and the words move slow;
Not so, when swift Camilla scours the plain,
Flies o'er th' unbending corn, and skims along the main.
Hear how Timotheus' varied lays surprise,
And bid alternate passions fall and rise!
While, at each change, the son of Libyan Jove
Now burns with glory, and then melts with love;
Now his fierce eyes with sparkling fury glow,
Now sighs steal out, and tears begin to flow:
Persians and Greeks like turns of Nature found,   380
And the world's victor stood subdued by sound!
The power of music all our hearts allow,
And what Timotheus was, is DRYDEN now.

    Avoid extremes; and shun the fault of such,
Who still are pleased too little or too much.
At every trifle scorn to take offense,
That always shows great pride, or little sense;
Those heads, as stomachs, are not sure the best,
Which nauseate all, and nothing can digest.
Yet let not each gay turn thy rapture move;   390
For fools admire, but men of sense approve;
As things seem large which we through mists descry,
Dullness is ever apt to magnify.

    Some foreign writers, some our own despise;
The ancients only, or the moderns prize.
Thus wit, like faith, by each man is applied
To one small sect, and all are damned beside.
Meanly they seek the blessing to confine,
And force that sun but on a part to shine,
Which not alone the southern wit sublimes,   400
But ripens spirits in cold northern climes;
Which from the first has shone on ages past,
Enlights the present, and shall warm the last;
Though each may feel increases and decays,
And see now clearer and now darker days.
Regard not then if wit be old or new,
But blame the false, and value still the true.

    Some ne'er advance a judgment of their own,
But catch the spreading notion of the town;
They reason and conclude by precedent,   410

372 **Camilla** warlike queen in the *Aeneid* 374 **Timotheus'** Athe-
nian musician celebrated in Dryden's ode, *Alexander's Feast*
376 **son . . . Jove** Alexander the Great, who claimed divine
descent

And own stale nonsense which they ne'er invent.
Some judge of authors' names, not works, and then
Nor praise nor blame the writings, but the men.
Of all this servile herd, the worst is he
That in proud dullness joins with quality.
A constant critic at the great man's board,
To fetch and carry nonsense for my lord.
What woeful stuff this madrigal would be,
In some starved hackney sonneteer, or me?
But let a lord once own the happy lines,   420
How the wit brightens! how the style refines!
Before his sacred name flies every fault,
And each exalted stanza teems with thought!
   The vulgar thus through imitation err;
As oft the learned by being singular;
So much they scorn the crowd, that if the throng
By chance go right, they purposely go wrong:
So schismatics the plain believers quit,
And are but damned for having too much wit.
Some praise at morning what they blame at night;   430
But always think the last opinion right.
A Muse by these is like a mistress used,
This hour she's idolized, the next abused;
While their weak heads, like towns unfortified,
'Twixt sense and nonsense daily change their side.
Ask them the cause; they're wiser still, they say;
And still tomorrow's wiser than today.
We think our fathers fools, so wise we grow;
Our wiser sons, no doubt, will think us so.
Once school-divines this zealous isle o'erspread;   440
Who knew most sentences, was deepest read;
Faith, Gospel, all, seemed made to be disputed,
And none had sense enough to be confuted:
Scotists and Thomists, now, in peace remain,
Amidst their kindred cobwebs in Duck Lane.
If Faith itself has different dresses worn,
What wonder modes in wit should take their turn?
Oft, leaving what is natural and fit,
The current folly proves the ready wit;
And authors think their reputation safe,   450
Which lives as long as fools are pleased to laugh.
   Some valuing those of their own side or mind,
Still make themselves the measure of mankind:
Fondly we think we honor merit then,

445 **Duck Lane** region in London where second-hand books
were sold

When we but praise ourselves in other men.
Parties in wit attend on those of state,
And public faction doubles private hate.
Pride, malice, folly, against Dryden rose,
In various shapes of parsons, critics, beaus;
But sense survived, when merry jests were past;   460
For rising merit will buoy up at last.
Might he return, and bless once more our eyes,
New Blackmores and new Milbourns must arise:
Nay, should great Homer lift his awful head,
Zoilus again would start up from the dead.
Envy will merit, as its shade, pursue;
But like a shadow, proves the substance true;
For envied wit, like Sol eclipsed, makes known
Th' opposing body's grossness, not its own.
When first that sun too powerful beams displays,   470
It draws up vapors which obscure its rays;
But even those clouds at last adorn its way,
Reflect new glories, and augment the day.
   Be thou the first true merit to befriend;
His praise is lost, who stays till all commend.
Short is the date, alas! of modern rhymes,
And 'tis but just to let them live betimes.
No longer now that golden age appears,
When patriarch-wits survived a thousand years:
Now length of fame (our second life) is lost,   480
And bare threescore is all even that can boast;
Our sons their fathers' failing language see,
And such as Chaucer is, shall Dryden be.
So when the faithful pencil has designed
Some bright idea of the master's mind,
Where a new world leaps out at his command,
And ready Nature waits upon his hand;
When the ripe colors soften and unite,
And sweetly melt into just shade and light;
When mellow years their full perfection give,   490
And each bold figure just begins to live,
The treacherous colors the fair art betray,
And all the bright creation fades away!
   Unhappy wit, like most mistaken things,
Atones not for that envy which it brings.
In youth alone its empty praise we boast,

463 **Blackmores . . . Milbourns** writers who had belittled Dryden's poetry 465 **Zoilus** ancient author of a carping commentary on Homer

But soon the short-lived vanity is lost:
Like some fair flower the early spring supplies,
That gaily blooms, but even in blooming dies.
What is this wit, which must our cares employ?   500
The owner's wife, that other men enjoy;
Then most our trouble still when most admired,
And still the more we give, the more required;
Whose fame with pains we guard, but lose with ease,
Sure some to vex, but never all to please;
'Tis what the vicious fear, the virtuous shun,
By fools 'tis hated, and by knaves undone!
   If wit so much from ignorance undergo,
Ah let not learning too commence its foe!
Of old, those met rewards who could excel,   510
And such were praised who but endeavored well:
Though triumphs were to generals only due,
Crowns were reserved to grace the soldiers too.
Now, they who reach Parnassus' lofty crown,
Employ their pains to spurn some others down;
And while self-love each jealous writer rules,
Contending wits become the sport of fools:
But still the worst with most regret commend,
For each ill author is as bad a friend.
To what base ends, and by what abject ways,   520
Are mortals urged through sacred lust of praise!
Ah ne'er so dire a thirst of glory boast,
Nor in the critic let the man be lost.
Good nature and good sense must ever join;
To err is human, to forgive, divine.
   But if in noble minds some dregs remain
Not yet purged off, of spleen and sour disdain;
Discharge that rage on more provoking crimes,
Nor fear a dearth in these flagitious times.
No pardon vile obscenity should find,   530
Though wit and art conspire to move your mind;
But dullness with obscenity must prove
As shameful sure as impotence in love.
In the fat age of pleasure, wealth, and ease,
Sprung the rank weed, and thrived with large increase:
When love was all an easy monarch's care;
Seldom at council, never in a war:
Jilts ruled the state, and statesmen farces writ;
Nay wits had pensions, and young lords had wit:
The fair sat panting at a courtier's play,   540
And not a mask went unimproved away:

The modest fan was lifted up no more,
And virgins smiled at what they blushed before.
The following license of a foreign reign
Did all the dregs of bold Socinus drain;
Then unbelieving priests reformed the nation,
And taught more pleasant methods of salvation;
Where Heaven's free subjects might their rights dispute,
Lest God Himself should seem too absolute:
Pulpits their sacred satire learned to spare,   550
And vice admired to find a flatterer there!
Encouraged thus, wit's Titans braved the skies,
And the press groaned with licensed blasphemies.
These monsters, critics! with your darts engage,
Here point your thunder, and exhaust your rage!
Yet shun their fault, who, scandalously nice,
Will needs mistake an author into vice;
All seems infected that th' infected spy,
As all looks yellow to the jaundiced eye.

PART III

Learn then what morals critics ought to show,   560
For 'tis but half a judge's task, to know.
'Tis not enough, taste, judgment, learning, join;
In all you speak, let truth and candor shine;
That not alone what to your sense is due
All may allow; but seek your friendship too.
    Be silent always when you doubt your sense;
And speak, though sure, with seeming diffidence:
Some positive, persisting fops we know,
Who, if once wrong, will needs be always so;
But you, with pleasure own your errors past,   570
And make each day a critic on the last.
    'Tis not enough your counsel still be true;
Blunt truths more mischief than nice falsehoods do;
Men must be taught as if you taught them not,
And things unknown proposed as things forgot.
Without good breeding, truth is disapproved;
That only makes superior sense beloved.
    Be niggards of advice on no pretense;
For the worst avarice is that of sense.
With mean complaisance ne'er betray your trust,   580
Nor be so civil as to prove unjust.
Fear not the anger of the wise to raise;

545 **Socinus** Sixteenth-century Italian theologian who denied the divinity of Christ

Those best can bear reproof, who merit praise.
  'Twere well might critics still this freedom take,
But Appius reddens at each word you speak,
And stares, tremendous, with a threatening eye,
Like some fierce tyrant in old tapestry.
Fear most to tax an honorable fool,
Whose right it is, uncensured, to be dull;
Such, without wit, are poets when they please,   590
As without learning they can take degrees.
Leave dangerous truths to unsuccessful satires,
And flattery to fulsome dedicators,
Whom, when they praise, the world believes no more,
Than when they promise to give scribbling o'er.
'Tis best sometimes your censure to restrain,
And charitably let the dull be vain:
Your silence there is better than your spite,
For who can rail so long as they can write?
Still humming on, their drowsy course they keep,   600
And lashed so long, like tops, are lashed asleep.
False steps but help them to renew the race,
As, after stumbling, jades will mend their pace.
What crowds of these, impenitently bold,
In sounds and jingling syllables grown old,
Still run on poets in a raging vein,
Even to the dregs and squeezings of the brain,
Strain out the last dull dropping of their sense,
And rhyme with all the rage of impotence!
  Such shameless bards we have; and yet 'tis true,   610
There are as mad, abandoned critics too.
The bookful blockhead, ignorantly read,
With loads of learnèd lumber in his head,
With his own tongue still edifies his ears,
And always listening to himself appears.
All books he reads, and all he reads assails,
From Dryden's Fables down to Durfey's Tales.
With him, most authors steal their works, or buy;
Garth did not write his own Dispensary.
Name a new play, and he's the poet's friend,   620
Nay showed his faults—but when would poets mend?
No place so sacred from such fops is barred,

585 **Appius** John Dennis, irascible contemporary critic, author
of an unsuccessful tragedy, *Appius and Virginia* 617 **Durfey's**
Tom Durfey (1653-1723), writer of poems, tales, and plays
619 **Garth** Sir Samuel Garth (1661-1719), author of the bur-
lesque poem, *The Dispensary*

Nor is Paul's church more safe than Paul's churchyard
Nay, fly to altars; there they'll talk you dead:
For fools rush in where angels fear to tread.
Distrustful sense with modest caution speaks,
It still looks home, and short excursions makes;
But rattling nonsense in full volleys breaks,
And never shocked, and never turned aside,
Bursts out, resistless, with a thundering tide.   630
　　But where's the man who counsel can bestow,
Still pleased to teach, and yet not proud to know?
Unbiassed, or by favor, or by spite;
Not dully prepossessed, nor blindly right;
Though learned, well-bred; and though well-bred, sincere;
Modestly bold, and humanly severe:
Who to a friend his faults can freely show,
And gladly praise the merit of a foe?
Blessed with a taste exact, yet unconfined;
A knowledge both of books and human kind;   640
Generous converse; a soul exempt from pride;
And love to praise, with reason on his side?
　　Such once were critics; such the happy few,
Athens and Rome in better ages knew.
The mighty Stagirite first left the shore,
Spread all his sails, and durst the deeps explore;
He steered securely, and discovered far,
Led by the light of the Maeonian star.
Poets, a race long unconfined, and free,
Still fond and proud of savage liberty,   650
Received his laws; and stood convinced 'twas fit,
Who conquered Nature, should preside o'er wit.
　　Horace still charms with graceful negligence,
And without method talks us into sense,
Will, like a friend, familiarly convey
The truest notions in the easiest way.
He, who supreme in judgment, as in wit,
Might boldly censure, as he boldly writ,
Yet judged with coolness, though he sung with fire;
His precepts teach but what his works inspire.   660
Our critics take a contrary extreme,
They judge with fury, but they write with phlegm:
Nor suffers Horace more in wrong translations
By wits, than critics in as wrong quotations.
　　See Dionysius Homer's thoughts refine,

648 **Maeonian star** Homer   665 **Dionysius** of Helicarnassus,
Greek rhetorician

And call new beauties forth from every line!
   Fancy and art in gay Petronius please,
The scholar's learning, with the courtier's ease.
   In grave Quintilian's copious work, we find
The justest rules, and clearest method joined: 670
Thus useful arms in magazines we place,
All ranged in order, and disposed with grace,
But less to please the eye, than arm the hand,
Still fit for use, and ready at command.
   Thee, bold Longinus! all the Nine inspire,
And bless their critic with a poet's fire.
An ardent judge, who, zealous in his trust,
With warmth gives sentence, yet is always just;
Whose own example strengthens all his laws;
And is himself that great sublime he draws.   680
   Thus long succeeding critics justly reigned,
License repressed, and useful laws ordained.
Learning and Rome alike in empire grew;
And arts still followed where her eagles flew;
From the same foes, at last, both felt their doom,
And the same age saw learning fall, and Rome.
With tyranny, then superstition joined,
As that the body, this enslaved the mind;
Much was believed, but little understood,
And to be dull was construed to be good;   690
A second deluge learning thus o'errun,
And the monks finished what the Goths begun.
   At length Erasmus, that great injured name,
(The glory of the priesthood, and the shame!)
Stemmed the wild torrent of a barbarous age,
And drove those holy Vandals off the stage.
   But see! each Muse, in Leo's golden days,
Starts from her trance, and trims her withered bays;
Rome's ancient genius, o'er its ruins spread,
Shakes off the dust, and rears his reverend head.   700
Then sculpture and her sister-arts revive;
Stones leaped to form, and rocks began to live;
With sweeter notes each rising temple rung;
A Raphael painted, and a Vida sung.

667 Petronius author of the Latin *Satyricon,* a satirical tale containing passages of criticism **669 Quintilian** Roman author of the *Institutes of Oratory* **675 Longinus** Greek author of the treatise *On the Sublime* **the Nine** the nine Muses **697 Leo's** Pope Leo X (1475-1521), patron of scholarship and the arts **704 Vida** sixteenth-century Italian scholar, critic, and poet

Immortal Vida: on whose honored brow
The poet's bays and critic's ivy grow:
Cremona now shall ever boast thy name,
As next in place to Mantua, next in fame!
  But soon by impious arms from Latium chased,
Their ancient bounds the banished Muses passed;   710
Thence arts o'er all the northern world advance,
But critic-learning flourished most in France:
The rules a nation, born to serve, obeys;
And Boileau still in right of Horace sways.
But we, brave Britons, foreign laws despised,
And kept unconquered, and uncivilized;
Fierce for the liberties of wit, and bold,
We still defied the Romans, as of old.
Yet some there were, among the sounder few
Of those who less presumed, and better knew,   720
Who durst assert the juster ancient cause,
And here restored wit's fundamental laws.
Such was the Muse, whose rules and practice tell,
"Nature's chief masterpiece is writing well."
Such was Roscommon, not more learned than good,
With manners generous as his noble blood;
To him the wit of Greece and Rome was known,
And every author's merit, but his own.
Such late was Walsh—the Muse's judge and friend,
Who justly knew to blame or to commend;   730
To failings mild, but zealous for desert;
The clearest head, and the sincerest heart.
This humble praise, lamented shade! receive,
This praise at least a grateful Muse may give:
The Muse, whose early voice you taught to sing,
Prescribed her heights, and pruned her tender wing,
(Her guide now lost) no more attempts to rise,
But in low numbers short excursions tries:
Content, if hence th' unlearned their wants may view,
The learned reflect on what before they knew: 740
Careless of censure, nor too fond of fame;
Still pleased to praise, yet not afraid to blame;

714 **Boileau** (1636-1711), author of *L'art poétique*, which, with Vida's *De arte poetica*, is in the line of development between Horace's *Ars poetica* and Pope's present essay 724 "Nature's . . ." quoted from the Duke of Buckingham's *Essay on Poetry* 725 **Roscommon** author, in 1684, of an *Essay on Translated Verse* 729 **Walsh** William Walsh (1663-1708), critic and poet, Pope's early friend and literary adviser

Averse alike to flatter, or offend;
Not free from faults, nor yet too vain to mend.

1711

The Rape of the Lock

AN HEROI-COMICAL POEM

Nolueram, Belinda, tuos violare capillos;
Sed juvat, hoc precibus me tribuisse tuis.—MARTIAL

TO MRS. ARABELLA FERMOR

MADAM,—It will be in vain to deny that I have some regard
for this piece, since I dedicate it to you. Yet you may bear me
witness, it was intended only to divert a few young ladies,
who have good sense and good humor enough to laugh not only
at their sex's little unguarded follies, but at their own. But as
it was communicated with the air of a secret, it soon found its
way into the world. An imperfect copy having been offered to
a bookseller, you had the good nature for my sake to consent
to the publication of one more correct: this I was forced to
before I had executed half my design, for the machinery was
entirely wanting to complete it.

The machinery, Madam, is a term invented by the critics, to
signify that part which the deities, angels, or daemons are made
to act in a poem: for the ancient poets are in one respect like
many modern ladies: let an action be never so trivial in itself,
they always make it appear of the utmost importance. These
machines I determined to raise on a very new and odd foun-
dation, the Rosicrucian doctrine of spirits.

I know how disagreeable it is to make use of hard words
before a lady; but 'tis so much the concern of a poet to have
his works understood, and particularly by your sex, that you
must give me leave to explain two or three difficult terms.

The Rosicrucians are a people I must bring you acquainted
with. The best account I know of them is in a French book
called *Le Comte de Gabalis,* which, both in its title and size is
so like a novel that many of the fair sex have read it for one
by mistake. According to these gentlemen, the four elements
are inhabited by spirits, which they call sylphs, gnomes,
nymphs and salamanders. The gnomes, or daemons of earth,
delight in mischief; but the sylphs, whose habitation is in the
air, are the best-conditioned creatures imaginable. For they say,
any mortals may enjoy the most intimate familiarities with
these gentle spirits, upon a condition very easy to all true
adepts, an inviolate preservation of chastity.

As to the following cantos, all the passages of them are as

Nolueram . . . tuis "I was reluctant, Belinda, to violate your
locks, but I am glad to have granted this to your prayers."

fabulous as the vision at the beginning, or the transformation
at the end; (except the loss of your hair, which I always
mention with reverence). The human persons are as fictitious
as the airy ones; and the character of Belinda, as it is now
managed, resembles you in nothing but in beauty.

If this poem had as many graces as there are in your person,
or in your mind, yet I could never hope it should pass through
the world half so uncensured as you have done. But let its
fortune be what it will, mine is happy enough, to have given
me this occasion of assuring you that I am, with the truest
esteem, Madam, your most obedient, humble servant,

A. POPE

CANTO I

WHAT dire offense from amorous causes springs,
What mighty contests rise from trivial things,
I sing—This verse to CARYLL, Muse! is due:
This, even Belinda may vouchsafe to view:
Slight is the subject, but not so the praise,
If she inspire, and he approve my lays.
    Say what strange motive, goddess! could compel
A well-bred lord t' assault a gentle belle?
O say what stranger cause, yet unexplored,
Could make a gentle belle reject a lord?   10
In tasks so bold, can little men engage,
And in soft bosoms dwells such mighty rage?
    Sol through white curtains shot a timorous ray,
And oped those eyes that must eclipse the day:
Now lap-dogs give themselves the rousing shake,
And sleepless lovers, just at twelve, awake:
Thrice rung the bell, the slipper knocked the ground,
And the pressed watch returned a silver sound.
Belinda still her downy pillow pressed,
Her guardian sylph prolonged the balmy rest: 20
'Twas he had summoned to her silent bed
The morning dream that hovered o'er her head;
A youth more glittering than a birth-night beau,
(That even in slumber caused her cheek to glow)
Seemed to her ear his winning lips to lay,
And thus in whispers said, or seemed to say.
    "Fairest of mortals, thou distinguished care
Of thousand bright inhabitants of air!

3 **Caryll** Pope's friend, at whose request this poem was written,
in the attempt to reconcile Miss Arabella Fermor to Caryll's
relative, Lord Petre

If e'er one vision touched thy infant thought,
Of all the nurse and all the priest have taught;   30
Of airy elves by moonlight shadows seen,
The silver token, and the circled green,
Or virgins visited by angel powers,
With golden crowns and wreaths of heavenly flowers;
Hear and believe! thy own importance know,
Nor bound thy narrow views to things below.
Some secret truths, from learnèd pride concealed,
To maids alone and children are revealed:
What though no credit doubting wits may give?
The fair and innocent shall still believe.   40
Know, then, unnumbered spirits round thee fly,
The light militia of the lower sky:
These, though unseen, are ever on the wing,
Hang o'er the box, and hover round the ring.
Think what an equipage thou hast in air,
And view with scorn two pages and a chair.
As now your own, our beings were of old,
And once inclosed in woman's beauteous mold;
Thence, by a soft transition, we repair
From earthly vehicles to these of air.   50
Think not, when woman's transient breath is fled,
That all her vanities at once are dead;
Succeeding vanities she still regards,
And though she plays no more, o'erlooks the cards.
Her joy in gilded chariots, when alive,
And love of ombre, after death survive.
For when the fair in all their pride expire,
To their first elements their souls retire:
The sprites of fiery termagants in flame
Mount up, and take a salamander's name.   60
Soft yielding minds to water glide away,
And sip, with nymphs, their elemental tea.
The graver prude sinks downward to a gnome,
In search of mischief still on earth to roam.
The light coquettes in sylphs aloft repair,
And sport and flutter in the fields of air.
    "Know farther yet; whoever fair and chaste
Rejects mankind, is by some sylph embraced:
For spirits, freed from mortal laws, with ease
Assume what sexes and what shapes they please.   70
What guards the purity of melting maids,
In courtly balls, and midnight masquerades,
Safe from the treacherous friend, the daring spark,

The glance by day, the whisper in the dark,
When kind occasion prompts their warm desires,
When music softens, and when dancing fires?
'Tis but their sylph, the wise celestials know,
Though honor is the word with men below.
   "Some nymphs there are, too conscious of their face,
For life predestined to the gnomes' embrace.   80
These swell their prospects and exalt their pride,
When offers are disdained, and love denied:
Then gay ideas crowd the vacant brain,
While peers, and dukes, and all their sweeping train,
And garters, stars, and coronets appear,
And in soft sounds, 'Your Grace' salutes their ear.
'Tis these that early taint the female soul,
Instruct the eyes of young coquettes to roll,
Teach infant cheeks a bidden blush to know,
And little hearts to flutter at a beau.   90
   "Oft when the world imagine women stray,
The sylphs through mystic mazes guide their way,
Through all the giddy circle they pursue,
And old impertinence expel by new.
What tender maid but must a victim fall
To one man's treat, but for another's ball?
When Florio speaks, what virgin could withstand,
If gentle Damon did not squeeze her hand?
With varying vanities, from every part,
They shift the moving toyshop of their heart;   100
Where wigs with wigs, with sword-knots sword-knots
    strive,
Beaux banish beaux, and coaches coaches drive.
This erring mortals levity may call,
Oh blind to truth! the sylphs contrive it all.
   "Of these am I, who thy protection claim,
A watchful sprite, and Ariel is my name.
Late, as I ranged the crystal wilds of air,
In the clear mirror of thy ruling star
I saw, alas! some dread event impend,
Ere to the main this morning sun descend,   110
But heaven reveals not what, or how, or where:
Warned by the sylph, oh pious maid, beware!
This to disclose is all thy guardian can:
Beware of all, but most beware of man!"
   He said; when Shock, who thought she slept too long,
Leaped up, and waked his mistress with his tongue.
'Twas then, Belinda, if report say true,

Thy eyes first opened on a billet-doux;
Wounds, charms, and ardors, were no sooner read,
But all the vision vanished from thy head.   120
   And now, unveiled, the toilet stands displayed,
Each silver vase in mystic order laid.
First, robed in white, the nymph intent adores,
With head uncovered, the cosmetic powers.
A heavenly image in the glass appears,
To that she bends, to that her eye she rears;
Th' inferior priestess, at her altar's side,
Trembling, begins the sacred rites of pride.
Unnumbered treasures ope at once, and here
The various offerings of the world appear;   130
From each she nicely culls with curious toil,
And decks the goddess with the glittering spoil.
This casket India's glowing gems unlocks,
And all Arabia breathes from yonder box.
The tortoise here and elephant unite,
Transformed to combs, the speckled and the white.
Here files of pins extend their shining rows,
Puffs, powders, patches, Bibles, billet-doux.
Now awful beauty puts on all its arms;
The fair each moment rises in her charms,   140
Repairs her smiles, awakens every grace,
And calls forth all the wonders of her face;
Sees by degrees a purer blush arise,
And keener lightnings quicken in her eyes.
The busy sylphs surround their darling care,
These set the head, and those divide the hair,
Some fold the sleeve, while others plait the gown;
And Betty's praised for labors not her own.

CANTO II

Not with more glories, in th' ethereal plain,
The sun first rises o'er the purpled main,
Than, issuing forth, the rival of his beams
Launched on the bosom of the silver Thames.
Fair nymphs, and well-dressed youths around her shone,
But every eye was fixed on her alone.
On her white breast a sparkling cross she wore,
Which Jews might kiss, and infidels adore.
Her lively looks a sprightly mind disclose,
Quick as her eyes, and as unfixed as those: 10
Favors to none, to all she smiles extends;
Oft she rejects, but never once offends.

Bright as the sun, her eyes the gazers strike,
And, like the sun, they shine on all alike.
Yet graceful ease, and sweetness void of pride,
Might hide her faults, if belles had faults to hide:
If to her share some female errors fall,
Look on her face, and you'll forget 'em all.
   This nymph, to the destruction of mankind,
Nourished two locks, which graceful hung behind   20
In equal curls, and well conspired to deck
With shining ringlets the smooth ivory neck.
Love in these labyrinths his slaves detains,
And mighty hearts are held in slender chains.
With hairy springes we the birds betray,
Slight lines of hair surprise the finny prey,
Fair tresses man's imperial race ensnare,
And beauty draws us with a single hair.
   Th' adventurous baron the bright locks admired;
He saw, he wished, and to the prize aspired.   30
Resolved to win, he meditates the way,
By force to ravish, or by fraud betray;
For when success a lover's toils attends,
Few ask, if fraud or force attained his ends.
   For this, ere Phoebus rose, he had implored
Propitious Heaven, and every power adored,
But chiefly Love—to Love an altar built,
Of twelve vast French romances, neatly gilt.
There lay three garters, half a pair of gloves;
And all the trophies of his former loves;   40
With tender billet-doux he lights the pyre,
And breathes three amorous sighs to raise the fire.
Then prostrate falls, and begs with ardent eyes
Soon to obtain, and long possess the prize:
The powers gave ear, and granted half his prayer,
The rest, the winds dispersed in empty air.
   But now secure the painted vessel glides,
The sunbeams trembling on the floating tides:
While melting music steals upon the sky,
And softened sounds along the waters die;   50
Smooth flow the waves, the zephyrs gently play,
Belinda smiled, and all the world was gay.
All but the sylph—with careful thoughts oppressed,
Th' impending woe sat heavy on his breast.
He summons straight his denizens of air;
The lucid squadrons round the sails repair:

25 springes traps, snares

Soft o'er the shrouds aërial whispers breathe,
That seemed but zephyrs to the train beneath.
Some to the sun their insect-wings unfold,
Waft on the breeze, or sink in clouds of gold;   60
Transparent forms, too fine for mortal sight,
Their fluid bodies half dissolved in light.
Loose to the wind their airy garments flew,
Thin glittering textures of the filmy dew,
Dipped in the richest tincture of the skies,
Where light disports in ever-mingling dyes,
While every beam new transient colors flings,
Colors that change whene'er they wave their wings.
Amid the circle, on the gilded mast,
Superior by the head, was Ariel placed;   70
His purple pinions opening to the sun,
He raised his azure wand, and thus begun.
    "Ye sylphs and sylphids, to your chief give ear,
Fays, fairies, genii, elves, and daemons, hear!
Ye know the spheres and various tasks assigned
By laws eternal to th' aërial kind.
Some in the fields of purest ether play,
And bask and whiten in the blaze of day.
Some guide the course of wandering orbs on high,
Or roll the planets through the boundless sky.   80
Some less refined, beneath the moon's pale light,
Pursue the stars that shoot athwart the night,
Or suck the mists in grosser air below,
Or dip their pinions in the painted bow,
Or brew fierce tempests on the wintry main,
Or o'er the glebe distil the kindly rain.
Others on earth o'er human race preside,
Watch all their ways, and all their actions guide:
Of these the chief the care of nations own,
And guard with arms divine the British throne.   90
    "Our humbler province is to tend the fair,
Not a less pleasing, though less glorious care;
To save the powder from too rude a gale,
Nor let the imprisoned essences exhale;
To draw fresh colors from the vernal flowers;
To steal from rainbows ere they drop in showers
A brighter wash; to curl their waving hairs,
Assist their blushes, and inspire their airs;
Nay oft, in dreams, invention we bestow,
To change a flounce, or add a furbelow.   100

86 glebe soil

"This day, black omens threat the brightest fair
That e'er deserved a watchful spirit's care;
Some dire disaster, or by force, or slight;
But what, or where, the Fates have wrapped in night.
Whether the nymph shall break Diana's law,
Or some frail china jar receive a flaw,
Or stain her honor, or her new brocade;
Forget her prayers, or miss a masquerade;
Or lose her heart, or necklace, at a ball;
Or whether Heaven has doomed that Shock must fall.
Haste, then, ye spirits! to your charge repair: 111
The fluttering fan be Zephyretta's care;
The drops to thee, Brillante, we consign;
And, Momentilla, let the watch be thine;
Do thou, Crispissa, tend her favorite lock;
Ariel himself shall be the guard of Shock.
    "To fifty chosen sylphs, of special note,
We trust th' important charge, the petticoat:
Oft have we known that sevenfold fence to fail,
Though stiff with hoops, and armed with ribs of
            whale;   120
Form a strong line about the silver bound,
And guard the wide circumference around.
    "Whatever spirit, careless of his charge,
His post neglects, or leaves the fair at large,
Shall feel sharp vengeance soon o'ertake his sins,
Be stopped in vials, or transfixed with pins;
Or plunged in lakes of bitter washes lie,
Or wedged whole ages in a bodkin's eye:
Gums and pomatums shall his flight restrain,
While clogged he beats his silken wings in vain;   130
Or alum styptics with contracting power
Shrink his thin essence like a rivelled flower:
Or, as Ixion fixed, the wretch shall feel
The giddy motion of the whirling mill,
In fumes of burning chocolate shall glow,
And tremble at the sea that froths below!"
    He spoke; the spirits from the sails descend;
Some, orb in orb, around the nymph extend;
Some thrid the mazy ringlets of her hair;
Some hang upon the pendants of her ear: 140
With beating hearts the dire event they wait,
Anxious, and trembling for the birth of Fate.

CANTO III

CLOSE by those meads, for ever crowned with flowers,
Where Thames with pride surveys his rising towers,
There stands a structure of majestic frame,
Which from the neighboring Hampton takes its name.
Here Britain's statesmen oft the fall foredoom
Of foreign tyrants, and of nymphs at home;
Here thou, great ANNA! whom three realms obey,
Dost sometimes counsel take—and sometimes tea.
   Hither the heroes and the nymphs resort,
To taste awhile the pleasures of a court;   10
In various talk th' instructive hours they passed,
Who gave the ball, or paid the visit last;
One speaks the glory of the British Queen,
And one describes a charming Indian screen;
A third interprets motions, looks, and eyes;
At every word a reputation dies.
Snuff, or the fan, supply each pause of chat,
With singing, laughing, ogling, *and all that*.
   Meanwhile, declining from the noon of day,
The sun obliquely shoots his burning ray;   20
The hungry judges soon the sentence sign,
And wretches hang that jurymen may dine;
The merchant from th' exchange returns in peace,
And the long labors of the toilet cease.
Belinda now, whom thirst of fame invites,
Burns to encounter two adventurous knights,
At omber singly to decide their doom;
And swells her breast with conquests yet to come.
Straight the three bands prepare in arms to join,
Each band the number of the sacred nine.   30
Soon as she spreads her hand, th' aërial guard
Descend, and sit on each important card:
First Ariel perched upon a Matadore,
Then each, according to the rank they bore;
For sylphs, yet mindful of their ancient race,
Are, as when women, wondrous fond of place.
   Behold, four Kings in majesty revered,
With hoary whiskers and a forky beard;
And four fair Queens whose hands sustain a flower,

27 **omber** three-handed card game, popular at the time, introduced from Spain 33 **Matadore** The Aces of Spades and of Clubs, together with one other card varying with the trumps, were called "Matadores."

Th' expressive emblem of their softer power; **40**
Four Knaves in garbs succinct, a trusty band,
Caps on their heads, and halberts in their hand;
And particolored troops, a shining train,
Draw forth to combat on the velvet plain.
 The skilful nymph reviews her force with care:
"Let Spades be trumps!" she said, and trumps they were.
 Now move to war her sable Matadores,
In show like leaders of the swarthy Moors.
Spadillio first, unconquerable lord!
Led off two captive trumps, and swept the board. **50**
As many more Manillio forced to yield,
And marched a victor from the verdant field.
Him Basto followed, but his fate more hard
Gained but one trump and one plebeian card.
With his broad saber next, a chief in years,
The hoary Majesty of Spades appears,
Puts forth one manly leg, to sight revealed,
The rest, his many-colored robe concealed.
The rebel Knave, who dares his prince engage,
Proves the just victim of his royal rage. **60**
Even mighty Pam, that kings and queens o'erthrew
And mowed down armies in the fights of Lu,
Sad chance of war! now destitute of aid,
Falls undistinguished by the victor Spade!
 Thus far both armies to Belinda yield;
Now to the baron fate inclines the field.
His warlike Amazon her host invades,
Th' imperial consort of the crown of Spades.
The Club's black tyrant first her victim died,
Spite of his haughty mien, and barbarous pride: **70**
What boots the regal circle on his head,
His giant limbs, in state unwieldy spread;
That long behind he trails his pompous robe,
And, of all monarchs, only grasps the globe?
 The baron now his Diamonds pours apace;
Th' embroidered King who shows but half his face,
And his refulgent Queen, with powers combined
Of broken troops an easy conquest find.
Clubs, Diamonds, Hearts, in wild disorder seen,
With throngs promiscuous strow the level green. **80**
Thus when dispersed a routed army runs,
Of Asia's troops, and Afric's sable sons,

62 **Lu** another card game 80 **strow** old form of *strew*

With like confusion different nations fly,
Of various habit, and of various dye,
The pierced battalions disunited fall,
In heaps on heaps; one fate o'erwhelms them all.
 The Knave of Diamonds tries his wily arts,
And wins (oh shameful chance!) the Queen of Hearts.
At this, the blood the virgin's cheek forsook,
A livid paleness spreads o'er all her look;   90
She sees, and trembles at th' approaching ill,
Just in the jaws of ruin, and codille.
And now (as oft in some distempered state)
On one nice trick depends the general fate.
An Ace of Hearts steps forth: the King unseen
Lurked in her hand, and mourned his captive Queen:
He springs to vengeance with an eager pace,
And falls like thunder on the prostrate Ace.
The nymph exulting fills with shouts the sky;
The walls, the woods, and long canals reply.   100
 Oh thoughtless mortals! ever blind to fate,
Too soon dejected, and too soon elate.
Sudden, these honors shall be snatched away,
And cursed for ever this victorious day.
 For lo! the board with cups and spoons is crowned,
The berries crackle, and the mill turns round;
On shining altars of Japan they raise
The silver lamp; the fiery spirits blaze:
From silver spouts the grateful liquors glide,
While China's earth receives the smoking tide: 110
At once they gratify their scent and taste,
And frequent cups prolong the rich repast.
Straight hover round the fair her airy band;
Some, as she sipped, the fuming liquor fanned,
Some o'er her lap their careful plumes displayed,
Trembling, and conscious of the rich brocade.
Coffee (which makes the politician wise,
And see through all things with his half-shut eyes)
Sent up in vapors to the baron's brain
New stratagems, the radiant lock to gain.   120
Ah cease, rash youth! desist ere 'tis too late,
Fear the just gods, and think of Scylla's fate!
Changed to a bird, and sent to flit in air,

92 **codille** signifies that an opponent has won the game 122-4
Scylla . . . Nisus' Scylla betrayed her father, Nisus, by cutting
off a lock of his hair on which depended his life and the safety
of his kingdom, and was turned into a bird.

She dearly pays for Nisus' injured hair!
But when to mischief mortals bend their will,
How soon they find fit instruments of ill!
Just then, Clarissa drew with tempting grace
A two-edged weapon from her shining case:
So ladies in romance assist their knight,
Present the spear, and arm him for the fight.   130
He takes the gift with reverence and extends
The little engine on his fingers' ends;
This just behind Belinda's neck he spread,
As o'er the fragrant steams she bends her head.
Swift to the lock a thousand sprites repair,
A thousand wings, by turns, blow back the hair;
And thrice they twitched the diamond in her ear;
Thrice she looked back, and thrice the foe drew near.
Just in that instant, anxious Ariel sought
The close recesses of the virgin's thought;   140
As on the nosegay in her breast reclined,
He watched th' ideas rising in her mind,
Sudden he viewed, in spite of all her art,
An earthly lover lurking at her heart.
Amazed, confused, he found his power expired,
Resigned to fate, and with a sigh retired.
    The peer now spreads the glittering forfex wide,
T' inclose the lock; now joins it, to divide.
Even then, before the fatal engine closed,
A wretched sylph too fondly interposed;   150
Fate urged the shears, and cut the sylph in twain,
(But airy substance soon unites again)
The meeting points the sacred hair dissever
From the fair head, for ever, and for ever!
    Then flashed the living lightning from her eyes,
And screams of horror rend th' affrighted skies.
Not louder shrieks to pitying Heaven are cast,
When husbands or when lap-dogs breathe their last;
Or when rich China vessels fallen from high,
In glittering dust and painted fragments lie!   160
    "Let wreaths of triumph now my temples twine"
(The victor cried) "the glorious prize is mine!
While fish in streams, or birds delight in air,
Or in a coach and six the British fair,
As long as *Atalantis* shall be read,
Or the small pillow grace a lady's bed,

165 **Atalantis** a scandal-mongering novel by Mrs. Manley, published in 1709

While visits shall be paid on solemn days,
When numerous wax lights in bright order blaze,
While nymphs take treats, or assignations give,
So long my honor, name, and praise shall live!   170
What time would spare, from steel receives its date,
And monuments, like men, submit to fate!
Steel could the labor of the gods destroy,
And strike to dust th' imperial towers of Troy;
Steel could the works of mortal pride confound,
And hew triumphal arches to the ground.
What wonder then, fair nymph! thy hairs should feel
The conquering force of unresisted steel?"

CANTO IV

BUT anxious cares the pensive nymph oppressed,
And secret passions labored in her breast.
Not youthful kings in battle seized alive,
Not scornful virgins who their charms survive,
Not ardent lovers robbed of all their bliss,
Not ancient ladies when refused a kiss,
Not tyrants fierce that unrepenting die,
Not Cynthia when her manteau's pinned awry,
E'er felt such rage, resentment, and despair,
As thou, sad virgin! for thy ravished hair.   10
   For, that sad moment, when the sylphs withdrew,
And Ariel weeping from Belinda flew,
Umbriel, a dusky, melancholy sprite,
As ever sullied the fair face of light,
Down to the central earth, his proper scene,
Repaired to search the gloomy Cave of Spleen.
   Swift on his sooty pinions flits the gnome,
And in a vapor reached the dismal dome.
No cheerful breeze this sullen regions knows,
The dreaded east is all the wind that blows.   20
Here in a grotto, sheltered close from air,
And screened in shades from day's detested glare,
She sighs for ever on her pensive bed,
Pain at her side, and Megrim at her head.
   Two handmaids wait the throne: alike in place,
But differing far in figure and in face.
Here stood Ill-nature like an ancient maid,
Her wrinkled form in black and white arrayed;
With store of prayers, for mornings, nights, and noons,

24 Megrim migraine, head-ache

Her hand is filled; her bosom with lampoons.   30
   There Affectation, with a sickly mien,
Shows in her cheek the roses of eighteen,
Practiced to lisp, and hang the head aside,
Faints into airs, and languishes with pride,
On the rich quilt sinks with becoming woe,
Wrapped in a gown, for sickness, and for show.
The fair ones feel such maladies as these,
When each new night dress gives a new disease.
   A constant vapor o'er the palace flies;
Strange phantoms rising as the mists arise;   40
Dreadful, as hermit's dreams in haunted shades,
Or bright, as visions of expiring maids.
Now glaring fiends, and snakes on rolling spires,
Pale specters, gaping tombs, and purple fires:
Now lakes of liquid gold, Elysian scenes,
And crystal domes, and angels in machines.
   Unnumbered throngs on every side are seen
Of bodies changed to various forms by Spleen.
Here living teapots stand, one arm held out,
One bent; the handle this, and that the spout: 50
A pipkin there, like Homer's tripod walks;
Here sighs a jar, and there a goose pie talks;
Men prove with child, as powerful fancy works,
And maids turned bottles, call aloud for corks.
   Safe passed the gnome through this fantastic band,
A branch of healing spleenwort in his hand.
Then thus addressed the power: "Hail, wayward Queen!
Who rule the sex to fifty from fifteen:
Parent of vapors, and of female wit,
Who give th' hysteric or poetic fit,   60
On various tempers act by various ways,
Make some take physic, others scribble plays;
Who cause the proud their visits to delay,
And send the godly in a pet to pray.
A nymph there is, that all thy power disdains,
And thousands more in equal mirth maintains.
But oh! if e'er thy gnome could spoil a grace,
Or raise a pimple on a beauteous face,
Like citron waters matrons' cheeks inflame,
Or change complexions at a losing game;   70
If e'er with airy horns I planted heads,
Or rumpled petticoats, or tumbled beds,
Or caused suspicion when no soul was rude,
Or discomposed the headdress of a prude,

Or e'er to costive lap dog gave disease,
Which not the tears of brightest eyes could ease:
Hear me, and touch Belinda with chagrin,
That single act gives half the world the spleen."
   The Goddess with a discontented air
Seems to reject him, though she grants his prayer.   80
A wondrous bag with both her hands she binds,
Like that where once Ulysses held the winds;
There she collects the force of female lungs,
Sighs, sobs, and passions, and the war of tongues.
A vial next she fills with fainting fears,
Soft sorrows, melting griefs, and flowing tears.
The gnome rejoicing bears her gifts away,
Spreads his black wings, and slowly mounts to day.
   Sunk in Thalestris' arms the nymph he found,
Her eyes dejected and her hair unbound.   90
Full o'er their heads the swelling bag he rent,
And all the furies issued at the vent.
Belinda burns with more than mortal ire,
And fierce Thalestris fans the rising fire.
"O wretched maid!" she spread her hands, and cried,
(While Hampton's echoes, "Wretched maid!" replied)
"Was it for this you took such constant care
The bodkin, comb, and essence to prepare?
For this your locks in paper durance bound,
For this with torturing irons wreathed around?   100
For this with fillets strained your tender head,
And bravely bore the double loads of lead?
Gods! shall the ravisher display your hair,
While the fops envy and the ladies stare!
Honor forbid! at whose unrivaled shrine
Ease, pleasure, virtue, all our sex resign.
Methinks already I your tears survey,
Already hear the horrid things they say,
Already see you a degraded toast,
And all your honor in a whisper lost!   110
How shall I, then, your helpless fame defend?
'Twill then be infamy to seem your friend!
And shall this prize, th' inestimable prize,
Exposed through crystal to the gazing eyes,
And heightened by the diamond's circling rays,
On that rapacious hand for ever blaze?
Sooner shall grass in Hyde Park Circus grow,

117 **Hyde Park Circus** worn by the heavy carriage traffic

And wits take lodgings in the sound of Bow;
Sooner let earth, air, sea, to chaos fall,
Men, monkeys, lap dogs, parrots, perish all!"   120
    She said; then raging to Sir Plume repairs,
And bids her beau demand the precious hairs:
(Sir Plume of amber snuffbox justly vain,
And the nice conduct of a clouded cane)
With earnest eyes, and round unthinking face,
He first the snuffbox opened, then the case,
And thus broke out—"My Lord, why, what the devil?
Z—ds! damn the lock! 'fore Gad, you must be civil!
Plague on't! 'tis past a jest—nay prithee, pox!
Give her the hair"—he spoke, and rapped his box.   130
"It grieves me much" (replied the peer again)
"Who speaks so well should ever speak in vain,
But by this lock, this sacred lock I swear,
(Which never more shall join its parted hair;
Which never more its honors shall renew,
Clipped from the lovely head where late it grew)
That while my nostrils draw the vital air,
This hand, which won it, shall for ever wear."
He spoke, and speaking, in proud triumph spread
The long-contended honors of her head.   140
    But Umbriel, hateful gnome! forbears not so;
He breaks the vial whence the sorrows flow.
Then see! the nymph in beauteous grief appears,
Her eyes half-languishing, half-drowned in tears;
On her heaved bosom hung her drooping head,
Which, with a sigh, she raised; and thus she said:
"For ever cursed be this detested day,
Which snatched my best, my favorite curl away!
Happy! ah ten times happy had I been,
If Hampton Court these eyes had never seen!   150
Yet am I not the first mistaken maid,
By love of courts to numerous ills betrayed.
Oh had I rather unadmired remained
In some lone isle, or distant northern land;
Where the gilt chariot never marks the way,
Where none learn omber, none e'er taste bohea!
There kept my charms concealed from mortal eye,

118 **sound of Bow** within hearing of the bells of Bow Church,
in Cheapside, the mercantile part of London 121 **Sir Plume** "Sir
George Brown. He was angry that the poet should make him
talk nothing but nonsense"—WARBURTON. 156 **bohea** variety
of China tea

Like roses that in deserts bloom and die.
What moved my mind with youthful lords to roam?
Oh had I stayed, and said my prayers at home!   160
'Twas this, the morning omens seemed to tell:
Thrice from my trembling hand the patchbox fell;
The tottering china shook without a wind,
Nay, Poll sat mute, and Shock was most unkind!
A sylph too warned me of the threats of fate,
In mystic visions, now believed too late!
See the poor remnants of these slighted hairs!
My hands shall rend what even thy rapine spares:
These in two sable ringlets taught to break,
Once gave new beauties to the snowy neck;   170
The sister-lock now sits uncouth, alone,
And in its fellow's fate foresees its own;
Uncurled it hangs, the fatal shears demands,
And tempts, once more, thy sacrilegious hands.
Oh hadst thou, cruel! been content to seize
Hairs less in sight, or any hairs but these!"

CANTO V

SHE said: the pitying audience melt in tears.
But fate and love had stopped the baron's ears.
In vain Thalestris with reproach assails,
For who can move when fair Belinda fails?
Not half so fixed the Trojan could remain,
While Anna begged and Dido raged in vain.
Then grave Clarissa graceful waved her fan;
Silence ensued, and thus the nymph began.
  "Say, why are beauties praised and honored most,
The wise man's passion, and the vain man's toast?   10
Why decked with all that land and sea afford,
Why angels called, and angel-like adored?
Why round our coaches crowd the white-gloved beaux,
Why bows the side-box from its inmost rows?
How vain are all these glories, all our pains,
Unless good sense preserve what beauty gains:
That men may say, when we the front-box grace,
'Behold the first in virtue as in face!'
Oh! if to dance all night, and dress all day,
Charmed the smallpox, or chased old age away;   20
Who would not scorn what housewife's cares produce,
Or who would learn one earthly thing of use?
To patch, nay ogle, might become a saint,

5 the Trojan Aeneas, in Virgil's *Aeneid*, Book IV

Nor could it sure be such a sin to paint.
But since, alas! frail beauty must decay,
Curled or uncurled, since locks will turn to grey;
Since painted, or not painted, all shall fade,
And she who scorns a man, must die a maid;
What then remains, but well our power to use,
And keep good-humor still whate'er we lose?   30
And trust me, dear! good-humor can prevail,
When airs, and flights, and screams, and scolding fail.
Beauties in vain their pretty eyes may roll;
Charms strike the sight, but merit wins the soul."
   So spoke the dame, but no applause ensued;
Belinda frowned, Thalestris called her prude.
"To arms, to arms!" the fierce virago cries,
And swift as lightning to the combat flies.
All side in parties, and begin th' attack:
Fans clap, silks rustle, and tough whalebones crack;   40
Heroes' and heroines' shouts confusedly rise,
And bass, and treble voices strike the skies.
No common weapons in their hands are found,
Like gods they fight, nor dread a mortal wound.
   So when bold Homer makes the gods engage,
And heavenly breasts with human passions rage;
'Gainst Pallas, Mars; Latona, Hermes arms;
And all Olympus rings with loud alarms:
Jove's thunder roars, Heaven trembles all around,
Blue Neptune storms, the bellowing deeps resound: 50
Earth shakes her nodding towers, the ground gives way,
And the pale ghosts start at the flash of day!
   Triumphant Umbriel on a sconce's height
Clapped his glad wings, and sate to view the fight:
Propped on their bodkin spears, the sprites survey
The growing combat, or assist the fray.
   While through the press enraged Thalestris flies,
And scatters death around from both her eyes,
A beau and witling perished in the throng,
One died in metaphor, and one in song.   60
"O cruel nymph! a living death I bear,"
Cried Dapperwit, and sunk beside his chair.
A mournful glance Sir Fopling upwards cast,
"Those eyes are made so killing"—was his last.
Thus on Maeander's flowery margin lies
Th' expiring swan, and as he sings he dies.
   When bold Sir Plume had drawn Clarissa down,
Chloe stepped in, and killed him with a frown;

She smiled to see the doughty hero slain,
But, at her smile, the beau revived again. 70
   Now Jove suspends his golden scales in air,
Weighs the men's wits against the lady's hair;
The doubtful beam long nods from side to side;
At length the wits mount up, the hairs subside.
   See fierce Belinda on the baron flies,
With more than usual lightning in her eyes:
Nor feared the chief th' unequal fight to try,
Who sought no more than on his foe to die.
But this bold lord with manly strength endued,
She with one finger and a thumb subdued: 80
Just where the breath of life his nostrils drew,
A charge of snuff the wily virgin threw;
The gnomes direct, to every atom just,
The pungent grains of titillating dust.
Sudden, with starting tears each eye o'erflows,
And the high dome re-echoes to his nose.
   "Now meet thy fate," incensed Belinda cried,
And drew a deadly bodkin from her side.
(The same, his ancient personage to deck,
Her great-great-grandsire wore about his neck, 90
In three seal rings; which after, melted down,
Formed a vast buckle for his widow's gown:
Her infant grandame's whistle next it grew,
The bells she jingled, and the whistle blew;
Then in a bodkin graced her mother's hairs,
Which long she wore, and now Belinda wears.)
   "Boast not my fall" (he cried) "insulting foe!
Thou by some other shalt be laid as low.
Nor think, to die dejects my lofty mind:
All that I dread is leaving you behind! 100
Rather than so, ah let me still survive,
And burn in Cupid's flames—but burn alive."
   "Restore the lock!" she cries; and all around
"Restore the lock!" the vaulted roofs rebound.
Not fierce Othello in so loud a strain
Roared for the handkerchief that caused his pain.
But see how oft ambitious aims are crossed,
And chiefs contend till all the prize is lost!
The lock, obtained with guilt, and kept with pain,
In every place is sought, but sought in vain: 110
With such a prize no mortal must be blest,
So Heaven decrees! with Heaven who can contest?
   Some thought it mounted to the lunar sphere,

Since all things lost on earth are treasured there.
There heroes' wits are kept in ponderous vases,
And beaux' in snuff-boxes and tweezer-cases.
There broken vows, and deathbed alms are found,
And lovers' hearts with ends of riband bound,
The courtier's promises, and sick man's prayers,
The smiles of harlots, and the tears of heirs,   120
Cages for gnats, and chains to yoke a flea,
Dried butterflies, and tomes of casuistry.
    But trust the Muse—she saw it upward rise,
Though marked by none but quick, poetic eyes:
(So Rome's great founder to the heavens withdrew,
To Proculus alone confessed in view)
A sudden star, it shot through liquid air,
And drew behind a radiant trail of hair.
Not Berenice's lock first rose so bright,
The heavens bespangling with disheveled light.   130
The sylphs behold it kindling as it flies,
And pleased pursue its progress through the skies.
    This the beau monde shall from the Mall survey,
And hail with music its propitious ray.
This the blest lover shall for Venus take,
And send up vows from Rosamonda's lake.
This Partridge soon shall view in cloudless skies,
When next he looks through Galileo's eyes;
And hence th' egregious wizard shall foredoom
The fate of Louis, and the fall of Rome.   140
    Then cease, bright nymph! to mourn thy ravished hair,
Which adds new glory to the shining sphere!
Not all the tresses that fair head can boast
Shall draw such envy as the lock you lost.
For, after all the murders of your eye,
When, after millions slain, yourself shall die;
When those fair suns shall set, as set they must,
And all those tresses shall be laid in dust;

125 **Rome's great founder** According to Livy, Romulus, the
founder of Rome, was translated to heaven, and later appeared
in a vision to Proculus. 129 **Berenice's** A lock of Berenice's hair,
having disappeared mysteriously, was discovered transformed
into a constellation. 133 **the Mall** fashionable promenade in
London 136 **Rosamonda's lake** pond in St. James's Park, Lon-
don 137 **Partridge** John Partridge, a London astrologer who had
predicted each year the downfall of the Pope and the King of
France

This lock, the Muse shall consecrate to fame,
And 'midst the stars inscribe Belinda's name.   **150**

1712-1714

Elegy

TO THE MEMORY OF AN UNFORTUNATE LADY

WHAT beckoning ghost, along the moonlight shade
Invites my steps, and points to yonder glade?
'Tis she!—but why that bleeding bosom gored,
Why dimly gleams the visionary sword?
Oh ever beauteous, ever friendly! tell,
Is it, in heaven, a crime to love too well?
To bear too tender, or too firm a heart,
To act a lover's or a Roman's part?
Is there no bright reversion in the sky,
For those who greatly think, or bravely die?   10
    Why bade ye else, ye powers! her soul aspire
Above the vulgar flight of low desire?
Ambition first sprung from your blest abodes;
The glorious fault of angels and of gods:
Thence to their images on earth it flows,
And in the breast of kings and heroes glows.
Most souls, 'tis true, but peep out once an age,
Dull sullen prisoners in the body's cage:
Dim lights of life, that burn a length of years,
Useless, unseen, as lamps in sepulchers;   20
Like Eastern kings a lazy state they keep,
And close confined to their own palace, sleep.
    From these perhaps (ere nature bade her die)
Fate snatched her early to the pitying sky.
As into air the purer spirits flow,
And separate from their kindred dregs below;
So flew the soul to its congenial place,
Nor left one virtue to redeem her race.
    But thou, false guardian of a charge too good,
Thou, mean deserter of thy brother's blood!   30
See on these ruby lips the trembling breath,
These cheeks, now fading at the blast of death;
Cold is that breast which warmed the world before,
And those love-darting eyes must roll no more.
Thus, if eternal justice rules the ball,

Thus shall your wives, and thus your children fall:
On all the line a sudden vengeance waits,
And frequent hearses shall besiege your gates.
There passengers shall stand, and pointing say,
(While the long funerals blacken all the way)   40
Lo these were they, whose souls the Furies steeled,
And cursed with hearts unknowing how to yield.
Thus unlamented pass the proud away,
The gaze of fools, and pageant of a day!
So perish all, whose breast ne'er learned to glow
For others' good, or melt at others' woe.

　　What can atone (oh ever-injured shade!)
Thy fate unpitied, and thy rites unpaid?
No friend's complaint, no kind domestic tear
Pleased thy pale ghost, or graced thy mournful bier. 50
By foreign hands thy dying eyes were closed,
By foreign hands thy decent limbs composed,
By foreign hands thy humble grave adorned,
By strangers honored, and by strangers mourned!
What though no friends in sable weeds appear,
Grieve for an hour, perhaps, then mourn a year,
And bear about the mockery of woe
To midnight dances, and the public show?
What though no weeping loves thy ashes grace,
Nor polished marble emulate thy face?   60
What though no sacred earth allow thee room,
Nor hallowed dirge be muttered o'er thy tomb?
Yet shall thy grave with rising flowers be dressed,
And the green turf lie lightly on thy breast:
There shall the morn her earliest tears bestow,
There the first roses of the year shall blow;
While angels with their silver wings o'ershade
The ground, now sacred by thy relics made.

　　So peaceful rests, without a stone, a name,
What once had beauty, titles, wealth, and fame.   70
How loved, how honored once, avails thee not,
To whom related, or by whom begot;
A heap of dust alone remains of thee,
'Tis all thou art, and all the proud shall be!

　　Poets themselves must fall, like those they sung,
Deaf the praised ear, and mute the tuneful tongue.
Even he, whose soul now melts in mournful lays,
Shall shortly want the generous tear he pays;

78 want lack, need

Then from his closing eyes thy form shall part,
And the last pang shall tear thee from his heart, 80
Life's idle business at one gasp be o'er,
The Muse forgot, and thou beloved no more!

1717

An Essay on Man

EPISTLE I

ARGUMENT

OF THE NATURE AND STATE OF MAN WITH RESPECT TO THE UNIVERSE

Of man in the abstract.—I. That we can judge only with regard to our own system, being ignorant of the relation of systems and things. II. That man is not to be deemed imperfect, but a being suited to his place and rank in the creation, agreeable to the general order of things, and comformable to ends and relations to him unknown. III. That it is partly upon his ignorance of future events, and partly upon the hope of a future state, that all his happiness in the present depends. IV. The pride of aiming at more knowledge, and pretending to more perfection, the cause of man's error and misery. The impiety of putting himself in the place of God, and judging of the fitness or unfitness, perfection or imperfection, justice or injustice, of his dispensations. V. The absurdity of conceiving himself the final cause of the creation, or expecting that perfection in the moral world, which is not in the natural. VI. The unreasonableness of his complaints against Providence, while on the one hand he demands the perfections of the angels and on the other the bodily qualifications of the brutes; though, to possess any of the sensitive faculties in a higher degree, would render him miserable. VII. That throughout the whole visible world, an universal order and gradation in the sensual and mental faculties is observed, which causes a subordination of creature to creature, and of all creatures to Man. The gradations of sense, instinct, thought, reflection, reason; that reason alone countervails all the other faculties. VIII. How much further this order and subordination of living creatures may extend, above and below us; were any part of which broken, not that part only, but the whole connected creation must be destroyed. IX. The extravagance, madness, and pride of such a desire. X. The consequence of all, the absolute submission due to Providence, both as to our present and future state.

AWAKE, my St. John! leave all meaner things
To low ambition, and the pride of kings.
Let us (since life can little more supply
Than just to look about us and to die)
Expatiate free o'er all this scene of man;
A mighty maze! but not without a plan;
A wild, where weeds and flowers promiscuous shoot;
Or garden, tempting with forbidden fruit.
Together let us beat this ample field,
Try what the open, what the covert yield;   10
The latent tracts, the giddy heights explore
Of all who blindly creep, or sightless soar;
Eye Nature's walks, shoot folly as it flies,
And catch the manners living as they rise;
Laugh where we must, be candid where we can;
But vindicate the ways of God to man.
    I. Say first, of God above, or man below,
What can we reason, but from what we know?
Of man, what see we but his station here,
From which to reason, or to which refer?   20
Through worlds unnumbered though the God be known,
'Tis ours to trace him only in our own.
He, who through vast immensity can pierce,
See worlds on worlds compose one universe,
Observe how system into system runs,
What other planets circle other suns,
What varied being peoples every star,
May tell why Heaven has made us as we are.
But of this frame the bearings, and the ties,
The strong connections, nice dependencies,   30
Gradations just, has thy pervading soul
Looked through? or can a part contain the whole?
    Is the great chain, that draws all to agree,
And drawn supports, upheld by God, or thee?
    II. Presumptuous man! the reason wouldst thou find,
Why formed so weak, so little, and so blind?
First, if thou canst, the harder reason guess,
Why formed no weaker, blinder, and no less?
Ask of thy mother earth, why oaks are made
Taller and stronger than the weeds they shade?   40
Or ask of yonder argent fields above,

1 **St. John** Henry St. John, Viscount Bolingbroke, who encour-
aged this undertaking, and was to some extent Pope's philosophi-
cal mentor 16 **But vindicate** Cf. *Paradise Lost*, I, 26: "And
justify the ways of God to men."

Why Jove's satellites are less than Jove?
　Of systems possible, if 'tis confessed
That wisdom infinite must form the best,
Where all must fall or not coherent be,
And all that rises, rise in due degree;
Then, in the scale of reasoning life, 'tis plain,
There must be, somewhere, such a rank as man:
And all the question (wrangle e'er so long)
Is only this, if God has placed him wrong?　　　**50**
　Respecting man, whatever wrong we call,
May, must be right, as relative to all.
In human works, though labored on with pain,
A thousand movements scarce one purpose gain;
In God's, one single can its end produce;
Yet serves to second too some other use.
So man, who here seems principal alone,
Perhaps acts second to some sphere unknown,
Touches some wheel, or verges to some goal;
'Tis but a part we see, and not a whole.　　　**60**
　When the proud steed shall know why man restrains
His fiery course, or drives him o'er the plains;
When the dull ox, why now he breaks the clod,
Is now a victim, and now Egypt's god:
Then shall man's pride and dullness comprehend
His actions', passions', being's, use and end;
Why doing, suffering, checked, impelled; and why
This hour a slave, the next a deity.
　Then say not man's imperfect, Heaven in fault;
Say rather, man's as perfect as he ought:　　　**70**
His knowledge measured to his state and place;
His time a moment, and a point his space.
If to be perfect in a certain sphere,
What matter, soon or late, or here or there?
The blest today is as completely so,
As who began a thousand years ago.
　III. Heaven from all creatures hides the book of fate,
All but the page prescribed, their present state:
From brutes what men, from men what spirits know:
Or who could suffer being here below?　　　**80**
The lamb thy riot dooms to bleed today,
Had he thy reason, would he skip and play?
Pleased to the last, he crops the flowery food,
And licks the hand just raised to shed his blood.
Oh blindness to the future! kindly given.
That each may fill the circle marked by Heaven:

Who sees with equal eye, as God of all,
A hero perish, or a sparrow fall,
Atoms or systems into ruin hurled,
And now a bubble burst, and now a world.   90
    Hope humbly then; with trembling pinions soar;
Wait the great teacher death; and God adore.
What future bliss, He gives not thee to know,
But gives that hope to be thy blessing now.
Hope springs eternal in the human breast:
Man never is, but always to be blest:
The soul, uneasy and confined from home,
Rests and expatiates in a life to come.
    Lo, the poor Indian! whose untutored mind
Sees God in clouds, or hears Him in the wind;   100
His soul, proud science never taught to stray
Far as the solar-walk, or milky way;
Yet simple Nature to his hope has given,
Behind the cloud-topped hill, an humbler heaven;
Some safer world in depth of woods embraced,
Some happier island in the watery waste,
Where slaves once more their native land behold,
No fiends torment, no Christians thirst for gold.
To be, contents his natural desire,
He asks no angel's wings, no seraph's fire;   110
But thinks, admitted to that equal sky,
His faithful dog shall bear him company.
    IV. Go, wiser thou! and in thy scale of sense,
Weigh thy opinion against Providence;
Call imperfection what thou fanciest such,
Say, here He gives too little, there too much:
Destroy all creatures for thy sport or gust,
Yet cry, If man's unhappy, God's unjust;
If man alone engross not Heaven's high care,
Alone made perfect here, immortal there: 120
Snatch from his hand the balance and the rod,
Rejudge his justice, be the God of God.
In pride, in reasoning pride, our error lies;
All quit their sphere, and rush into the skies.
Pride still is aiming at the blessed abodes,
Men would be angels, angels would be gods.
Aspiring to be gods, if angels fell,
Aspiring to be angels, men rebel:
And who but wishes to invert the laws

117 **gust** taste, appetite

Of order, sins against th' Eternal Cause. 130
    V. Ask for what end the heavenly bodies shine,
Earth for whose use? Pride answers, " 'Tis for mine:
For me kind Nature wakes her genial power,
Suckles each herb, and spreads out every flower;
Annual for me, the grape, the rose renew,
The juice nectareous, and the balmy dew;
For me, the mine a thousand treasures brings;
For me, health gushes from a thousand springs;
Seas roll to waft me, suns to light me rise;
My footstool earth, my canopy the skies." 14C
    But errs not Nature from this gracious end,
From burning suns when livid deaths descend,
When earthquakes swallow, or when tempests sweep
Towns to one grave, whole nations to the deep?
"No" ('tis replied) "the first Almighty Cause
Acts not by partial, but by general laws;
Th' exceptions few; some change since all began:
And what created perfect?"—Why then man?
If the great end be human happiness,
Then Nature deviates; and can man do less? 150
As much that end a constant course requires
Of showers and sunshine, as of man's desires;
As much eternal springs and cloudless skies,
As men forever temperate, calm, and wise.
If plagues or earthquakes break not Heaven's design,
Why then a Borgia, or a Catiline?
Who knows but He, whose hand the lightning forms,
Who heaves old ocean, and who wings the storms;
Pours fierce ambition in a Caesar's mind,
Or turns young Ammon loose to scourge mankind? 160
From pride, from pride, our very reasoning springs;
Account for moral as for natural things:
Why charge we Heaven in those, in these acquit?
In both, to reason right is to submit.
    Better for us, perhaps, it might appear,
Were there all harmony, all virtue here;
That never air or ocean felt the wind;
That never passion discomposed the mind.
But all subsists by elemental strife;

142 **burning suns** It was believed that plagues are caused by
the midsummer sun. 156 **Borgia** Cesare Borgia (1476-1507),
notorious for his violence and crimes **Catiline** Roman conspira-
tor denounced by Cicero in several orations 160 **Ammon** Alex-
ander the Great

And passions are the elements of life.   170
The general order, since the whole began,
Is kept by Nature, and is kept in man.
    VI. What would this man? Now upward will he soar,
And little less than angel, would be more;
Now looking downwards, just as grieved appears,
To want the strength of bulls, the fur of bears.
Made for his use all creatures if he call,
Say what their use, had he the powers of all?
Nature to these, without profusion, kind,
The proper organs, proper powers assigned;   180
Each seeming want compensated of course,
Here with degrees of swiftness, there of force;
All in exact proportion to the state;
Nothing to add, and nothing to abate.
Each beast, each insect, happy in its own:
Is Heaven unkind to man, and man alone?
Shall he alone, whom rational we call,
Be pleased with nothing, if not blessed with all?
    The bliss of man (could pride that blessing find)
Is not to act or think beyond mankind;   190
No powers of body or of soul to share,
But what his nature and his state can bear.
Why has not man a microscopic eye?
For this plain reason, man is not a fly.
Say what the use, were finer optics given,
To inspect a mite, not comprehend the heaven?
Or touch, if tremblingly alive all o'er,
To smart and agonize at every pore?
Or quick effluvia darting through the brain,
Die of a rose in aromatic pain?   200
If Nature thundered in his opening ears,
And stunned him with the music of the spheres,
How would he wish that Heaven had left him still
The whispering zephyr, and the purling rill?
Who finds not Providence all good and wise,
Alike in what it gives, and what it denies?
    VII. Far as creation's ample range extends,
The scale of sensual, mental powers ascends:
Mark how it mounts, to man's imperial race,
From the green myriads in the peopled grass: 210

194 **not a fly** Flies and other small creatures were believed to
have microscopic vision. 199 **effluvia** the streams of invisible
particles by which, according to Epicurean theory, odors com-
municate themselves

What modes of sight betwixt each wide extreme,
The mole's dim curtain, and the lynx's beam:
Of smell, the headlong lioness between,
And hound sagacious on the tainted green:
Of hearing, from the life that fills the flood,
To that which warbles through the vernal wood:
The spider's touch, how exquisitely fine!
Feels at each thread, and lives along the line:
In the nice bee, what sense so subtly true
From poisonous herbs extract the healing dew?   220
How instinct varies in the groveling swine,
Compared, half-reasoning elephant, with thine!
'Twixt that, and reason, what a nice barrier;
For ever separate, yet for ever near!
Remembrance and reflection how allied;
What thin partitions sense from thought divide:
And middle natures, how they long to join,
Yet never pass th' insuperable line!
Without this just gradation, could they be
Subjected, these to those, or all to thee?   230
The powers of all subdued by thee alone,
Is not thy reason all these powers in one?

    VIII. See, through this air, this ocean, and this earth,
All matter quick, and bursting into birth.
Above, how high, progressive life may go!
Around, how wide! how deep extend below!
Vast chain of being! which from God began,
Natures ethereal, human, angel, man,
Beast, bird, fish, insect, what no eye can see,
No glass can reach; from Infinite to thee,   240
From thee to nothing.—On superior powers
Were we to press, inferior might on ours:
Or in the full creation leave a void,
Where, one step broken, the great scale's destroyed:
From Nature's chain whatever link you strike,
Tenth, or ten thousandth, breaks the chain alike.
    And, if each system in gradation roll
Alike essential to th' amazing whole,
The least confusion but in one, not all

212 **lynx's beam** according to the ancient opinion that vision consists in rays beamed from the eye; also, that the lynx is the most sharp-sighted of creatures 213 **lioness** believed to possess a dull sense of smell 214 **sagacious** acute in perception **tainted** imbued with an animal scent 220 **healing dew** honey, which was used for medication

That system only, but the whole must fall.   250
Let earth unbalanced from her orbit fly,
Planets and suns run lawless through the sky;
Let ruling angels from their spheres be hurled,
Being on being wrecked, and world on world;
Heaven's whole foundations to their center nod,
And Nature tremble to the throne of God.
All this dread order break—for whom? for thee?
Vile worm!—oh madness! pride! impiety!
    IX. What if the foot, ordained the dust to tread,
Or hand, to toil, aspired to be the head?   260
What if the head, the eye, or ear repined
To serve mere engines to the ruling mind?
Just as absurd for any part to claim
To be another, in this general frame:
Just as absurd, to mourn the tasks or pains,
The great directing Mind of all ordains.
    All are but parts of one stupendous whole,
Whose body Nature is, and God the soul;
That, changed through all, and yet in all the same;
Great in the earth, as in th' ethereal frame;   270
Warms in the sun, refreshes in the breeze,
Glows in the stars, and blossoms in the trees,
Lives through all life, extends through all extent,
Spreads undivided, operates unspent;
Breathes in our soul, informs our mortal part,
As full, as perfect, in a hair as heart;
As full, as perfect, in vile man that mourns,
As the rapt seraph that adores and burns:
To Him no high, no low, no great, no small;
He fills, He bounds, connects, and equals all.   280
    X. Cease then, nor order imperfection name:
Our proper bliss depends on what we blame.
Know thy own point: this kind, this due degree
Of blindness, weakness, Heaven bestows on thee.
Submit.—In this, or any other sphere,
Secure to be as blessed as thou canst bear:
Safe in the hand of one disposing Power,
Or in the natal, or the mortal hour.
All Nature is but art, unknown to thee;
All chance, direction, which thou canst not see;   290
All discord, harmony not understood;
All partial evil, universal good:
And, spite of pride, in erring reason's spite,
One truth is clear, Whatever is, is right.

EPISTLE II

ARGUMENT

OF THE NATURE AND STATE OF MAN WITH RESPECT
TO HIMSELF, AS AN INDIVIDUAL

I. The business of man not to pry into God, but to study him-
self. His middle nature; his powers and frailties. The limits of
his capacity. II. The two principles of man, self-love and rea-
son, both necessary. Self-love the stronger, and why. Their end
the same. III. The passions, and their use. The predominant
passion, and its force. Its necessity, in directing men to differ-
ent purposes. Its providential use, in fixing our principle, and
ascertaining our virtue. IV. Virtue and vice joined in our mixed
nature; the limits near, yet the things separate and evident:
what is the office of reason. V. How odious vice in itself, and
how we deceive ourselves into it. VI. That, however, the ends
of Providence and general good are answered in our passions
and imperfections. How usefully these are distributed to all
orders of men. How useful they are to society. And to the in-
dividuals. In every state, and every age of life.

I. Know then thyself, presume not God to scan,
The proper study of mankind is man.
Placed on this isthmus of a middle state,
A being darkly wise, and rudely great:
With too much knowledge for the sceptic side,
With too much weakness for the stoic's pride,
He hangs between; in doubt to act, or rest;
In doubt to deem himself a god, or beast;
In doubt his mind or body to prefer;
Born but to die, and reasoning but to err;   10
Alike in ignorance, his reason such,
Whether he thinks too little, or too much:
Chaos of thought and passion, all confused;
Still by himself abused, or disabused;
Created half to rise, and half to fall;
Great lord of all things, yet a prey to all;
Sole judge of truth, in endless error hurled:
The glory, jest, and riddle of the world!
    Go, wondrous creature! mount where science guides,
Go, measure earth, weigh air, and state the tides;   20
Instruct the planets in what orbs to run,
Correct old time, and regulate the sun;
Go, soar with Plato to th' empyreal sphere,
To the first good, first perfect, and first fair;

Or tread the mazy round his followers trod,
And quitting sense call imitating God;
As Eastern priests in giddy circles run,
And turn their heads to imitate the sun.
Go, teach Eternal Wisdom how to rule—
Then drop into thyself, and be a fool! 30

    Superior beings, when of late they saw
A mortal man unfold all nature's law,
Admired such wisdom in an earthly shape,
And showed a Newton as we show an ape.

    Could he, whose rules the rapid comet bind,
Describe or fix one movement of his mind?
Who saw its fires here rise, and there descend,
Explain his own beginning, or his end?
Alas what wonder! Man's superior part
Unchecked may rise, and climb from art to art; 40
But when his own great work is but begun,
What reason weaves, by passion is undone.

    Trace science then, with modesty thy guide;
First strip off all her equipage of pride;
Deduct but what is vanity, or dress,
Or learning's luxury, or idleness;
Or tricks to show the stretch of human brain,
Mere curious pleasure, or ingenious pain;
Expunge the whole, or lop th' excrescent parts
Of all our vices have created arts; 50
Then see how little the remaining sum,
Which served the past, and must the times to come!

    II. Two principles in human nature reign;
Self-love, to urge, and reason, to restrain;
Nor this a good, nor that a bad we call,
Each works its end, to move or govern all:
And to their proper operation still,
Ascribe all good; to their improper, ill.

    Self-love, the spring of motion, acts the soul;
Reason's comparing balance rules the whole. 60
Man, but for that, no action could attend,
And, but for this, were active to no end:
Fixed like a plant on his peculiar spot,
To draw nutrition, propagate, and rot:
Or, meteor-like, flame lawless through the void,
Destroying others, by himself destroyed.

    Most strength the moving principle requires;
Active its task, it prompts, impels, inspires.
Sedate and quiet the comparing lies,

Formed but to check, deliberate, and advise.   **70**
Self-love still stronger, as its objects nigh;
Reason's at distance, and in prospect lie:
That sees immediate good by present sense;
Reason, the future and the consequence.
Thicker than arguments, temptations throng,
At best more watchful this, but that more strong.
The action of the stronger to suspend
Reason still use, to reason still attend.
Attention, habit, and experience gains;
Each strengthens reason, and self-love restrains.   **80**
   Let subtle schoolmen teach these friends to fight,
More studious to divide than to unite;
And grace and virtue, sense and reason split,
With all the rash dexterity of wit.
Wits, just like fools, at war about a name,
Have full as oft no meaning, or the same.
Self-love and reason to one end aspire,
Pain their aversion, pleasure their desire;
But greedy that, its object would devour,
This taste the honey, and not wound the flower: **90**
Pleasure, or wrong or rightly understood,
Our greatest evil, or our greatest good.
   III. Modes of self-love the passions we may call:
'Tis real good, or seeming, moves them all:
But since not every good we can divide,
And reason bids us for our own provide;
Passions, though selfish, if their means be fair,
'List under reason, and deserve her care;
Those, that imparted, court a nobler aim,
Exalt their kind, and take some virtue's name.   **100**
   In lazy apathy let Stoics boast
Their virtue fixed; 'tis fixed as in a frost;
Contracted all, retiring to the breast;
But strength of mind is exercise, not rest:
The rising tempest puts in act the soul,
Parts it may ravage, but preserves the whole.
On life's vast ocean diversely we sail,
Reason the card, but passion is the gale;
Nor God alone in the still calm we find,
He mounts the storm, and walks upon the wind.   **110**
   Passions, like elements, though born to fight,
Yet, mixed and softened, in his work unite:

108 **card** on which are marked the points of the mariner's compass

These 'tis enough to temper and employ;
But what composes man, can man destroy?
Suffice that reason keep to Nature's road,
Subject, compound them, follow her and God.
Love, hope, and joy, fair pleasure's smiling train,
Hate, fear, and grief, the family of pain,
These mixed with art, and to due bounds confined,
Make and maintain the balance of the mind: 120
The lights and shades, whose well-accorded strife
Gives all the strength and color of our life.
    Pleasures are ever in our hands or eyes;
And when in act, they cease, in prospect, rise:
Present to grasp, and future still to find,
The whole employ of body and of mind.
All spread their charms, but charm not all alike;
On different senses different objects strike;
Hence different passions more or less inflame,
As strong or weak, the organs of the frame;   130
And hence one master passion in the breast,
Like Aaron's serpent, swallows up the rest.
    As man, perhaps, the moment of his breath
Receives the lurking principle of death;
The young disease, that must subdue at length,
Grows with his growth, and strengthens with his strength;
So, cast and mingled with his very frame,
The mind's disease, its ruling passion came;
Each vital humor which should feed the whole,
Soon flows to this, in body and in soul: 140
Whatever warms the heart, or fills the head,
As the mind opens, and its functions spread,
Imagination plies her dangerous art,
And pours it all upon the peccant part.
    Nature its mother, habit is its nurse;
Wit, spirit, faculties, but make it worse;
Reason itself but gives it edge and power;
As Heaven's blessed beam turns vinegar more sour.
    We, wretched subjects though to lawful sway,
In this weak queen, some favorite still obey: 150
Ah! if she lend not arms, as well as rules,
What can she more than tell us we are fools?
Teach us to mourn our nature, not to mend,
A sharp accuser, but a helpless friend!
Or from a judge turn pleader, to persuade

132 **Aaron's** The story of Aaron's rod is told in *Exodus* 7.10-12
144 **peccant** diseased

The choice we make, or justify it made;
Proud of an easy conquest all along,
She but removes weak passions for the strong:
So, when small humors gather to a gout,
The doctor fancies he has driven them out.   160
    Yes, Nature's road must ever be preferred;
Reason is here no guide, but still a guard:
'Tis hers to rectify, not overthrow,
And treat this passion more as friend than foe:
A mightier power the strong direction sends,
And several men impels to several ends:
Like varying winds, by other passions tossed,
This drives them constant to a certain coast.
Let power or knowledge, gold or glory, please,
Or (oft more strong than all) the love of ease;   170
Through life 'tis followed, even at life's expense;
The merchant's toil, the sage's indolence,
The monk's humility, the hero's pride,
All, all alike find reason on their side.
    Th' eternal art educing good from ill,
Grafts on this passion our best principle:
'Tis thus the mercury of man is fixed,
Strong grows the virtue with his nature mixed;
The dross cements what else were too refined,
And in one interest body acts with mind.   180
    As fruits, ungrateful to the planter's care,
On savage stocks inserted, learn to bear;
The surest virtues thus from passions shoot,
Wild Nature's vigor working at the root.
What crops of wit and honesty appear
From spleen, from obstinacy, hate, or fear!
See anger, zeal and fortitude supply;
Even avarice, prudence; sloth, philosophy;
Lust, through some certain strainers well refined,
Is gentle love, and charms all womankind;   190
Envy, to which the ignoble mind's a slave,
Is emulation in the learned or brave;
Nor virtue, male or female, can we name,
But what will grow on pride, or grow on shame.
    Thus Nature gives us (let it check our pride)
The virtue nearest to our vice allied:
Reason the bias turns to good from ill,
And Nero reigns a Titus, if he will.

198 **Titus** Roman Emperor, A.D. 79-81

The fiery soul abhorred in Catiline,
In Decius charms, in Curtius is divine: 200
The same ambition can destroy or save,
And makes a patriot as it makes a knave.
    IV. This light and darkness in our chaos joined,
What shall divide? The God within the mind.
    Extremes in nature equal ends produce,
In man they join to some mysterious use;
Though each by turns the other's bound invade,
As, in some well-wrought picture, light and shade,
And oft so mix, the difference is too nice
Where ends the virtue or begins the vice.   210
    Fools! who from hence into the notion fall,
That vice or virtue there is none at all.
If white and black blend, soften, and unite
A thousand ways, is there no black or white?
Ask your own heart, and nothing is so plain;
'Tis to mistake them, costs the time and pain.
    V. Vice is a monster of so frightful mien,
As, to be hated, needs but to be seen;
Yet seen too oft, familiar with her face,
We first endure, then pity, then embrace.   220
But where th' extreme of vice, was ne'er agreed:
Ask where's the north? at York, 'tis on the Tweed;
In Scotland, at the Orcades; and there,
At Greenland, Zembla, or the Lord knows where.
No creature owns it in the first degree,
But thinks his neighbor farther gone than he;
Even those who dwell beneath its very zone,
Or never feel the rage, or never own;
What happier natures shrink at with affright,
The hard inhabitant contends is right.   230
    VI. Virtuous and vicious every man must be,
Few in th' extreme, but all in the degree;
The rogue and fool by fits is fair and wise;
And even the best, by fits, what they despise.
'Tis but by parts we follow good or ill;
For, vice or virtue, self directs it still;
Each individual seeks a several goal;
But Heaven's great view is one, and that the whole.

200 **Decius** Roman Emperor, A.D. 249-51, who sacrificed his life
for a Roman victory **Curtius** legendary Roman hero, who leaped
into the chasm opened in the Forum by an earthquake 223
Orcades the Orkney Islands, off the northern coast of Scotland
224 Zembla Nova Zembla, in the Arctic Ocean, north of Russia

That counter-works each folly and caprice;
That disappoints th' effect of every vice;   240
That, happy frailties to all ranks applied;
Shame to the virgin, to the matron pride,
Fear to the statesman, rashness to the chief,
To kings presumption, and to crowds belief:
That, virtue's ends from vanity can raise,
Which seeks no interest, no reward but praise;
And build on wants, and on defects of mind,
The joy, the peace, the glory of mankind.
    Heaven forming each on other to depend,
A master, or a servant, or a friend,   250
Bids each on other for assistance call,
Till one man's weakness grows the strength of all.
Wants, frailties, passions, closer still ally
The common interest, or endear the tie.
To these we owe true friendship, love sincere,
Each homefelt joy that life inherits here;
Yet from the same we learn, in its decline,
Those joys, those loves, those interests to resign;
Taught half by reason, half by mere decay,
To welcome death, and calmly pass away.   260
    Whate'er the passion, knowledge, fame, or pelf,
Not one will change his neighbor with himself.
The learned is happy Nature to explore,
The fool is happy that he knows no more;
The rich is happy in the plenty given,
The poor contents him with the care of Heaven.
See the blind beggar dance, the cripple sing,
The sot a hero, lunatic a king;
The starving chemist in his golden views
Supremely blessed, the poet in his muse.   270
    See some strange comfort every state attend,
And pride bestowed on all, a common friend:
See some fit passion every age supply,
Hope travels through, nor quits us when we die.
    Behold the child, by Nature's kindly law,
Pleased with a rattle, tickled with a straw:
Some livelier plaything gives his youth delight,
A little louder, but as empty quite:
Scarfs, garters, gold, amuse his riper stage,
And beads and prayer books are the toys of age: 280
Pleased with this bauble still, as that before;
Till tired he sleeps, and life's poor play is o'er.
    Meanwhile opinion gilds with varying rays

Those painted clouds that beautify our days;
Each want of happiness by hope supplied,
And each vacuity of sense by pride:
These build as fast as knowledge can destroy;
In folly's cup still laughs the bubble, joy;
One prospect lost, another still we gain;
And not a vanity is given in vain;   290
Even mean self-love becomes, by force divine,
The scale to measure others' wants by thine.
See! and confess, one comfort still must rise,
'Tis this,—Though man's a fool, yet God is wise.

EPISTLE III

ARGUMENT

OF THE NATURE AND STATE OF MAN WITH RESPECT
TO SOCIETY

I. The whole universe one system of society. Nothing made
wholly for itself, nor yet wholly for another. The happiness of
animals mutual. II. Reason or instinct operate alike to the good
of each individual. Reason or instinct operate also to society, in
all animals. III. How far society carried by instinct. How much
farther by reason. IV. Of that which is called the state of na-
ture. Reason instructed by instinct in the invention of arts,
and in the forms of society. V. Origin of political societies.
Origin of monarchy. Patriarchal government. VI. Origin of true
religion and government, from the same principle, of love.
Origin of superstition and tyranny, from the same principle, of
fear. The influence of self-love operating to the social and pub-
lic good. Restoration of true religion and government on their
first principle. Mixed government. Various forms of each, and
the true end of all.

HERE then we rest: "The Universal Cause
Acts to one end, but acts by various laws."
In all the madness of superfluous health,
The train of pride, the impudence of wealth,
Let this great truth be present night and day;
But most be present, if we preach or pray.
  I. Look round our world; behold the chain of love
Combining all below and all above.
See plastic Nature working to this end,
The single atoms each to other tend,   10
Attract, attracted to, the next in place
Formed and impelled its neighbor to embrace

See matter next, with various life endued,
Press to one center still, the general good.
See dying vegetables life sustain,
See life dissolving vegetate again:
All forms that perish other forms supply,
(By turns we catch the vital breath, and die)
Like bubbles on the sea of matter born,
They rise, they break, and to that sea return.   20
Nothing is foreign: parts relate to whole;
One all-extending, all-preserving soul
Connects each being, greatest with the least;
Made beast in aid of man, and man of beast;
All served, all serving: nothing stands alone;
The chain holds on, and where it ends, unknown.

Has God, thou fool! worked solely for thy good,
Thy joy, thy pastime, thy attire, thy food?
Who for thy table feeds the wanton fawn,
For him as kindly spread the flowery lawn: 30
Is it for thee the lark ascends and sings?
Joy tunes his voice, joy elevates his wings.
Is it for thee the linnet pours his throat?
Loves of his own and raptures swell the note.
The bounding steed you pompously bestride,
Shares with his lord the pleasure and the pride.
Is thine alone the seed that strews the plain?
The birds of heaven shall vindicate their grain.
Thine the full harvest of the golden year?
Part pays, and justly, the deserving steer: 40
The hog, that ploughs not nor obeys thy call,
Lives on the labors of this lord of all.

Know, Nature's children shall divide her care;
The fur that warms a monarch, warmed a bear.
While man exclaims, "See all things for my use!"
"See man for mine!" replies a pampered goose:
And just as short of reason he must fall,
Who thinks all made for one, not one for all.

Grant that the powerful still the weak control;
Be man the wit and tyrant of the whole: 50
Nature that tyrant checks; he only knows,
And helps, another creature's wants and woes.
Say, will the falcon, stooping from above,
Smit with her varying plumage, spare the dove?
Admires the jay the insect's gilded wings?
Or hears the hawk when Philomela sings?

56 **Philomela** the nightingale

Man cares for all: to birds he gives his woods,
To beasts his pastures, and to fish his floods;
For some his interest prompts him to provide,
For more his pleasure, yet for more his pride: 60
All feed on one vain patron, and enjoy
Th' extensive blessing of his luxury.
That very life his learnèd hunger craves,
He saves from famine, from the savage saves;
Nay, feasts the animal he dooms his feast,
And till he ends the being, makes it blessed;
Which sees no more the stroke, or feels the pain,
Than favored man by touch ethereal slain.
The creature had his feast of life before;
Thou too must perish, when thy feast is o'er!   70
    To each unthinking being, Heaven a friend,
Gives not the useless knowledge of its end:
To man imparts it; but with such a view
As, while he dreads it, makes him hope it too:
The hour concealed, and so remote the fear,
Death still draws nearer, never seeming near.
Great standing miracle! that Heaven assigned
Its only thinking thing this turn of mind.
    II. Whether with reason, or with instinct blessed,
Know, all enjoy that power which suits them best;   80
To bliss alike by that direction tend,
And find the means proportioned to their end.
Say, where full instinct is th' unerring guide,
What pope or council can they need beside?
Reason, however able, cool at best,
Cares not for service, or but serves when pressed,
Stays till we call, and then not often near;
But honest instinct comes a volunteer,
Sure never to o'ershoot, but just to hit;
While still too wide or short is human wit;   90
Sure by quick nature happiness to gain,
Which heavier reason labors at in vain.
This too serves always, reason never long;
One must go right, the other may go wrong.
See then the acting and comparing powers
One in their nature, which are two in ours;
And reason raise o'er instinct as you can,
In this 'tis God directs, in that 'tis man.
    Who taught the nations of the field and wood

68 **favored man** alluding to the belief that men struck by light-
ning are recipients of divine favor

To shun their poison, and to choose their food?   100
Prescient, the tides or tempests to withstand,
Build on the wave, or arch beneath the sand?
Who made the spider parallels design,
Sure as De Moivre, without rule or line?
Who bade the stork, Columbus-like, explore
Heavens not his own, and worlds unknown before?
Who calls the council, states the certain day,
Who forms the phalanx, and who points the way?
   III. God, in the nature of each being, founds
Its proper bliss, and sets its proper bounds: 110
But as He framed a whole, the whole to bless,
On mutual wants built mutual happiness:
So from the first eternal Order ran,
And creature linked to creature, man to man.
Whate'er of life all-quickening ether keeps,
Or breathes through air, or shoots beneath the deeps,
Or pours profuse on earth, one nature feeds
The vital flame, and swells the genial seeds.
Not man alone, but all that roam the wood,
Or wing the sky, or roll along the flood,   120
Each loves itself, but not itself alone,
Each sex desires alike, till two are one.
Nor ends the pleasure with the fierce embrace;
They love themselves, a third time, in their race.
Thus beast and bird their common charge attend,
The mothers nurse it, and the sires defend;
The young dismissed to wander earth or air,
There stops the instinct, and there ends the care;
The link dissolves, each seeks a fresh embrace,
Another love succeeds, another race.   130
A longer care man's helpless kind demands;
That longer care contracts more lasting bands:
Reflection, reason, still the ties improve,
At once extend the interest, and the love;
With choice we fix, with sympathy we burn;
Each virtue in each passion takes its turn;
And still new needs, new helps, new habits rise,
That graft benevolence on charities.
Still as one brood, and as another rose,
These natural love maintained, habitual those: 140
The last, scarce ripened into perfect man,
Saw helpless him from whom their life began:

104 **De Moivre** Abraham De Moivre (1667-1754), eminent
French mathematician who settled in London

Memory and forecast just returns engage,
That pointed back to youth, this on to age;
While pleasure, gratitude, and hope, combined,
Still spread the interest, and preserved the kind.
    IV. Nor think, in Nature's state they blindly trod;
The state of Nature was the reign of God:
Self-love and social at her birth began,
Union the bond of all things, and of man.   150
Pride then was not; nor arts, that pride to aid;
Man walked with beast, joint tenant of the shade;
The same his table, and the same his bed;
No murder clothed him, and no murder fed.
In the same temple, the resounding wood,
All vocal beings hymned their equal God:
The shrine with gore unstained, with gold undressed,
Unbribed, unbloody, stood the blameless priest:
Heaven's attribute was universal care,
And man's prerogative to rule, but spare.   160
Ah! how unlike the man of times to come!
Of half that live the butcher and the tomb;
Who, foe to Nature, hears the general groan,
Murders their species, and betrays his own.
But just disease to luxury succeeds,
And every death its own avenger breeds;
The fury-passions from that blood began,
And turned on man, a fiercer savage, man.
    See him from Nature rising slow to art!
To copy instinct then was reason's part;   170
Thus then to man the voice of Nature spake—
"Go, from the creatures thy instructions take:
Learn from the birds what food the thickets yield;
Learn from the beasts the physic of the field;
Thy arts of building from the bee receive;
Learn of the mole to plough, the worm to weave;
Learn of the little nautilus to sail,
Spread the thin oar, and catch the driving gale.
Here too all forms of social union find,
And hence let reason, late, instruct mankind: 180
Here subterranean works and cities see;
There towns aerial on the waving tree.
Learn each small people's genius, policies,
The ant's republic, and the realm of bees;
How those in common all their wealth bestow,
And anarchy without confusion know;
And these for ever, though a monarch reign,

Their separate cells and properties maintain.
Mark what unvaried laws preserve each state,
Laws wise as Nature, and as fixed as fate.   190
In vain thy reason finer webs shall draw,
Entangle justice in her net of law,
And right, too rigid, harden into wrong;
Still for the strong too weak, the weak too strong.
Yet go! and thus o'er all the creatures sway,
Thus let the wiser make the rest obey;
And for those arts mere instinct could afford,
Be crowned as monarchs, or as gods adored."
  V. Great Nature spoke; observant man obeyed;
Cities were built, societies were made: 200
Here rose one little state; another near
Grew by like means, and joined, through love or fear.
Did here the trees with ruddier burdens bend,
And there the streams in purer rills descend?
What war could ravish, commerce could bestow,
And he returned a friend, who came a foe.
Converse and love mankind might strongly draw,
When love was liberty, and Nature law.
Thus states were formed; the name of king unknown,
Till common interest placed the sway in one.   210
'Twas virtue only (or in arts or arms,
Diffusing blessings, or averting harms)
The same which in a sire the sons obeyed,
A prince the father of a people made.
  VI. Till then, by Nature crowned, each patriarch sate,
King, priest, and parent of his growing state;
On him, their second Providence, they hung,
Their law his eye, their oracle his tongue.
He from the wondering furrow called the food,
Taught to command the fire, control the flood,   220
Draw forth the monsters of th' abyss profound,
Or fetch th' aerial eagle to the ground.
Till drooping, sickening, dying they began
Whom they revered as God to mourn as man:
Then, looking up from sire to sire, explored
One great first Father, and that first adored.
Or plain tradition that this all begun,
Conveyed unbroken faith from sire to son;
The worker from the work distinct was known,
And simple reason never sought but one: 230
Ere wit oblique had broke that steady light,
Man, like his Maker, saw that all was right;

To virtue, in the paths of pleasure, trod,
And owned a Father when he owned a God.
Love all the faith, and all th' allegiance then;
For Nature knew no right divine in men,
No ill could fear in God; and understood
A sovereign Being but a sovereign good.
True faith, true policy, united ran,
That was but love of God, and this of man.   240
    Who first taught souls enslaved, and realms undone,
Th' enormous faith of many made for one;
That proud exception to all Nature's laws,
T' invert the world, and counter-work its cause?
Force first made conquest, and that conquest, law;
Till superstition taught the tyrant awe,
Then shared the tyranny, then lent it aid,
And gods of conquerors, slaves of subjects made:
She midst the lightning's blaze, and thunder's sound,
When rocked the mountains, and when groaned the
        ground,   250
She taught the weak to bend, the proud to pray,
To power unseen, and mightier far than they:
She, from the rending earth and bursting skies,
Saw gods descend, and fiends infernal rise:
Here fixed the dreadful, there the blest abodes;
Fear made her devils, and weak hope her gods;
Gods partial, changeful, passionate, unjust,
Whose attributes were rage, revenge, or lust;
Such as the souls of cowards might conceive,
And, formed like tyrants, tyrants would believe.   260
Zeal then, not charity, became the guide;
And hell was built on spite, and heaven on pride.
Then sacred seemed th' ethereal vault no more;
Altars grew marble then, and reeked with gore:
Then first the flamen tasted living food;
Next his grim idol smeared with human blood;
With Heaven's own thunders shook the world below,
And played the god an engine on his foe.
    So drives self-love, through just and through unjust,
To one man's power, ambition, lucre, lust: 270
The same self-love, in all, becomes the cause
Of what restrains him, government and laws.
For, what one likes, if others like as well,

242 **enormous** in the old sense: abnormal, monstrous 265 **flamen**
a Roman priest, in the service of a particular god 268 **played
the god . . .** converted the god into an engine of war

What serves one will, when many wills rebel?
How shall he keep, what, sleeping or awake,
A weaker may surprize, a stronger take?
His safety must his liberty restrain:
All join to guard what each desires to gain.
Forced into virtue thus by self-defense,
Even kings learned justice and benevolence: 280
Self-love forsook the path it first pursued,
And found the private in the public good.
    'Twas then, the studious head or generous mind,
Follower of God, or friend of humankind,
Poet or patriot, rose but to restore
The faith and moral, Nature gave before;
Relumed her ancient light, not kindled new;
If not God's image, yet His shadow drew:
Taught power's due use to people and to kings,
Taught nor to slack, nor strain its tender strings,   290
The less, or greater, set so justly true,
That touching one must strike the other too;
Till jarring interests of themselves create
Th' according music of a well-mixed state.
Such is the world's great harmony, that springs
From order, union, full consent of things:
Where small and great, where weak and mighty, made
To serve, not suffer, strengthen, not invade;
More powerful each as needful to the rest,
And, in proportion as it blesses, blessed;
Draw to one point, and to one center bring
Beast, man, or angel, servant, lord, or king.
    For forms of government let fools contest;
Whate'er is best administered is best:
For modes of faith let graceless zealots fight;
His can't be wrong whose life is in the right:
In faith and hope the world will disagree,
But all mankind's concern is charity:
All must be false that thwart this one great end;
And all of God, that bless mankind or mend.   310
    Man, like the generous vine, supported lives;
The strength he gains is from th' embrace he gives.
On their own axis as the planets run,
Yet make at once their circle round the sun;
So two consistent motions act the soul;
And one regards itself, and one the whole.
    Thus God and Nature linked the general frame,
And bade self-love and social be the same.

EPISTLE IV

ARGUMENT

OF THE NATURE AND STATE OF MAN WITH RESPECT
TO HAPPINESS

I. False notions of happiness, philosophical and popular, an-
swered. II. It is the end of all men, and attainable by all. God
intends happiness to be equal; and to be so, it must be social,
since all particular happiness depends on general, and since He
governs by general, not particular, laws. As it is necessary for
order, and the peace and welfare of society, that external goods
should be unequal, happiness is not made to consist in these.
But, notwithstanding that inequality, the balance of happiness
among mankind is kept even by Providence, by the two pas-
sions of hope and fear. III. What the happiness of individuals
is, as far as is consistent with the constitution of this world;
and that the good man has here the advantage. The error of
imputing to virtue what are only the calamities of nature, or of
fortune. IV. The folly of expecting that God should alter his
general laws in favor of particulars. V. That we are not judges
who are good; but that, whoever they are, they must be hap-
piest. VI. That external goods are not the proper rewards, but
often inconsistent with, or destructive of virtue. That even these
can make no man happy without virtue: instanced in riches;
honors; nobility; greatness; fame; superior talents. With pic-
tures of human infelicity in men possessed of them all. VII.
That virtue only constitutes a happiness, whose object is uni-
versal, and whose prospect eternal. That the perfection of vir-
tue and happiness consists in a conformity to the order of
Providence here, and a resignation to it here and hereafter.

OH HAPPINESS! our being's end and aim!
Good, pleasure, ease, content! whate'er thy name:
That something still which prompts th' eternal sigh,
For which we bear to live, or dare to die,
Which still so near us, yet beyond us lies,
O'erlooked, seen double, by the fool and wise.
Plant of celestial seed! if dropped below,
Say, in what mortal soil thou deignst to grow?
Fair opening to some court's propitious shine,
Or deep with diamonds in the flaming mine?   10
Twined with the wreaths Parnassian laurels yield,
Or reaped in iron harvests of the field?
Where grows?—where grows it not? If vain our toil,
We ought to blame the culture, not the soil:
Fixed to no spot is happiness sincere,

'Tis nowhere to be found, or everywhere;
'Tis never to be bought, but always free,
And, fled from monarchs, St. John! dwells with thee.
   I. Ask of the learned the way? the learned are blind;
This bids to serve, and that to shun, mankind;   20
Some place the bliss in action, some in ease,
Those call it pleasure, and contentment these;
Some sunk to beasts, find pleasure end in pain;
Some swelled to gods, confess even virtue vain;
Or indolent, to each extreme they fall,
To trust in everything, or doubt of all.
   Who thus define it, say they more or less
Than this, that happiness is happiness?
   II. Take Nature's path, and mad opinion's leave;
All states can reach it, and all heads conceive;   30
Obvious her goods, in no extreme they dwell;
There needs but thinking right, and meaning well;
And, mourn our various portions as we please,
Equal is common sense, and common ease.
   Remember, man, "The Universal Cause
Acts not by partial, but by general laws";
And makes what happiness we justly call
Subsist not in the good of one, but all.
There's not a blessing individuals find,
But some way leans and hearkens to the kind: 40
No bandit fierce, no tyrant mad with pride,
No caverned hermit, rests self-satisfied:
Who most to shun or hate mankind pretend,
Seek an admirer, or would fix a friend:
Abstract what others feel, what others think,
All pleasures sicken, and all glories sink:
Each has his share; and who would more obtain,
Shall find, the pleasure pays not half the pain.
   Order is Heaven's first law; and, this confessed,
Some are, and must be, greater than the rest,   50
More rich, more wise; but who infers from hence
That such are happier, shocks all common sense.
Heaven to mankind impartial we confess,
If all are equal in their happiness:
But mutual wants this happiness increase;
All nature's difference keeps all nature's peace.
Condition, circumstance is not the thing;
Bliss is the same in subject or in king,
In who obtain defense, or who defend,
In him who is, or him who finds a friend: 60

Heaven breathes through every member of the whole
One common blessing, as one common soul.
But fortune's gifts if each alike possessed,
And each were equal, must not all contest?
If then to all men happiness was meant,
God in externals could not place content.

Fortune her gifts may variously dispose,
And these be happy called, unhappy those;
But Heaven's just balance equal will appear,
While those are placed in hope, and these in fear: 70
Not present good or ill, the joy or curse,
But future views of better, or of worse.

Oh sons of earth! attempt ye still to rise,
By mountains piled on mountains, to the skies?
Heaven still with laughter the vain toil surveys,
And buries madmen in the heaps they raise.

III. Know, all the good that individuals find,
Or God and Nature meant to mere mankind,
Reason's whole pleasure, all the joys of sense,
Lie in three words—health, peace, and competence.   80
But health consists with temperance alone;
And peace, O Virtue! peace is all thy own.
The good or bad the gifts of fortune gain;
But these less taste them, as they worse obtain.
Say, in pursuit of profit or delight,
Who risk the most, that take wrong means, or right?
Of vice or virtue, whether blessed or cursed,
Which meets contempt, or which compassion first?
Count all th' advantage prosperous vice attains,
'Tis but what virtue flies from and disdains: 90
And grant the bad what happiness they would,
One they must want, which is, to pass for good.

Oh blind to truth, and God's whole scheme below,
Who fancy bliss to vice, to virtue woe!
Who sees and follows that great scheme the best,
Best knows the blessing, and will most be blessed.
But fools, the good alone unhappy call,
For ills or accidents that chance to all.
See Falkland dies, the virtuous and the just!
See godlike Turenne prostrate on the dust!   100
See Sidney bleeds amid the martial strife!

99 **Falkland** statesman and man of letters; a Royalist, killed at
the battle of Newbury, 1643 100 **Turenne** Marshal in the
French army, killed in battle in 1675 101 **Sidney** the Eliza-
bethan Sir Philip Sidney, fatally wounded at Zutphen, in 1586

Was this their virtue, or contempt of life?
Say, was it virtue, more though Heaven ne'er gave,
Lamented Digby! sunk thee to the grave?
Tell me, if virtue made the son expire,
Why, full of days and honor, lives the sire?
Why drew Marseille's good bishop purer breath,
When Nature sickened, and each gale was death?
Or why so long (in life if long can be)
Lent Heaven a parent to the poor and me?   110
    What makes all physical or moral ill?
There deviates nature, and here wanders will.
God sends not ill; if rightly understood,
Or partial ill is universal good,
Or change admits, or Nature lets it fall;
Short, and but rare, 'til man improved it all.
We just as wisely might of Heaven complain
That righteous Abel was destroyed by Cain,
As that the virtuous son is ill at ease
When his lewd father gave the dire disease.   120
Think we, like some weak prince, th' Eternal Cause
Prone for His favorites to reverse His laws?
    IV. Shall burning Aetna, if a sage requires,
Forget to thunder, and recall her fires?
On air or sea new motions be impressed,
Oh blameless Bethel! to relieve thy breast?
When the loose mountain trembles from on high,
Shall gravitation cease, if you go by?
Or some old temple, nodding to its fall,
For Chartres' head reserve the hanging wall?   130
    V. But still this world (so fitted for the knave)
Contents us not. A better shall we have?
A kingdom of the just then let it be:
But first consider how those just agree.
The good must merit God's peculiar care;
But who, but God, can tell us who they are?
One thinks on Calvin Heaven's own spirit fell;
Another deems him instrument of hell;
If Calvin feel Heaven's blessing, or its rod,

104 **Digby** The Hon. Robert Digby, for whom Pope wrote an
epitaph in 1726 107 **good bishop** M. de Belsunce, who minis-
tered to the stricken at Marseille in the plague of 1720 110
parent Pope's mother died in 1733 at the age of 91. 123 **Aetna**
in whose crater Empedocles perished 126 **Bethel** Hugh Bethel,
Pope's close friend, who suffered from asthma 130 **Chartres'**
Francis Charteris (1675-1732), notorious debauchee and game-
ster

This cries, There is, and that, There is no God.   140
What shocks one part will edify the rest,
Nor with one system can they all be blessed.
The very best will variously incline,
And what rewards your virtue, punish mine.
Whatever is, is right.—This world, 'tis true,
Was made for Caesar—but for Titus too:
And which more blessed? who chained his country, say,
Or he whose virtue sighed to lose a day?
   "But sometimes virtue starves, while vice is fed."
What then? is the reward of virtue bread?   150
That, vice may merit, 'tis the price of toil;
The knave deserves it, when he tills the soil,
The knave deserves it, when he tempts the main,
Where folly fights for kings, or dives for gain.
The good man may be weak, be indolent;
Nor is his claim to plenty, but content.
But grant him riches, your demand is o'er?
"No—shall the good want health, the good want power?"
Add health, and power, and every earthly thing,
"Why bounded power? why private? why no king?"   160
Nay, why external for internal given?
Why is not man a god, and earth a heaven?
Who ask and reason thus, will scarce conceive
God gives enough, while he has more to give:
Immense the power, immense were the demand;
Say, at what part of nature will they stand?
   VI. What nothing earthly gives, or can destroy,
The soul's calm sunshine, and the heartfelt joy,
Is virtue's prize: a better would you fix?
Then give humility a coach and six,   170
Justice a conqueror's sword, or truth a gown,
Or public spirit its great cure, a crown.
Weak, foolish man! will Heaven reward us there
With the same trash mad mortals wish for here?
The boy and man an individual makes,
Yet sighst thou now for apples and for cakes?
Go, like the Indian, in another life,
Expect thy dog, thy bottle, and thy wife:
As well as dream such trifles are assigned,
As toys and empires, for a godlike mind.   180
Rewards, that either would to virtue bring
No joy, or be destructive of the thing:
How oft by these at sixty are undone
The virtues of a saint at twenty-one!

To whom can riches give repute, or trust,
Content, or pleasure, but the good and just?
Judges and senates have been bought for gold,
Esteem and love were never to be sold.
O fool! to think God hates the worthy mind,
The lover and the love of humankind, 190
Whose life is healthful, and whose conscience clear,
Because he wants a thousand pounds a year.

   Honor and shame from no condition rise;
Act well your part, there all the honor lies.
Fortune in men has some small difference made,
One flaunts in rags, one flutters in brocade;
The cobbler aproned, and the parson gowned,
The friar hooded, and the monarch crowned.
"What differ more" (you cry) "than crown and cowl?"
I'll tell you, friend! a wise man and a fool. 200
You'll find, if once the monarch acts the monk,
Or, cobbler-like, the parson will be drunk,
Worth makes the man, and want of it, the fellow;
The rest is all but leather or prunella.

   Stuck o'er with titles and hung round with strings,
That thou mayst be by kings or whores of kings.
Boast the pure blood of an illustrious race,
In quiet flow from Lucrece to Lucrece:
But by your father's worth if yours you rate,
Count me those only who were good and great. 210
Go! if your ancient but ignoble blood
Has crept through scoundrels ever since the flood,
Go! and pretend your family is young;
Nor own, your fathers have been fools so long.
What can ennoble sots, or slaves, or cowards?
Alas! not all the blood of all the Howards.

   Look next on greatness; say where greatness lies?
"Where, but among the heroes and the wise?"
Heroes are much the same, the point's agreed,
From Macedonia's madman to the Swede; 220
The whole strange purpose of their lives, to find
Or make an enemy of all mankind!
Not one looks backward, onward still he goes,
Yet ne'er looks forward farther than his nose.
No less alike the politic and wise;

204 **leather or prunella** the leather apron of the cobbler, and the
cloth of the parson's gown 216 **the Howards** an illustrious and
noble English family 220 **Macedonia's madman** Alexander the
Great **the Swede** Charles XII of Sweden

All sly slow things, with circumspective eyes:
Men in their loose unguarded hours they take,
Not that themselves are wise, but others weak.
But grant that those can conquer, these can cheat;
'Tis phrase absurd to call a villain great: 230
Who wickedly is wise, or madly brave,
Is but the more a fool, the more a knave.
Who noble ends by noble means obtains,
Or failing, smiles in exile or in chains,
Like good Aurelius let him reign, or bleed
Like Socrates, that man is great indeed.
    What's fame? A fancied life in others' breath,
A thing beyond us, even before our death.
Just what you hear, you have, and what's unknown
The same (my lord) if Tully's, or your own.   240
All that we feel of it begins and ends
In the small circle of our foes or friends;
To all beside as much an empty shade
An Eugene living, as a Caesar dead;
Alike or when, or where, they shone, or shine,
Or on the Rubicon, or on the Rhine.
A wit's a feather, and a chief's a rod;
An honest man's the noblest work of God.
Fame but from death a villain's name can save,
As justice tears his body from the grave;   250
When what t' oblivion better were resigned,
Is hung on high, to poison half mankind.
All fame is foreign, but of true desert;
Plays round the head, but comes not to the heart:
One self-approving hour whole years outweighs
Of stupid starers, and of loud huzzas;
And more true joy Marcellus exiled feels,
Than Caesar with a senate at his heels.
    In parts superior what advantage lies?
Tell (for you can) what is it to be wise?   260
'Tis but to know how little can be known;
To see all others' faults and feel our own:
Condemned in business or in arts to drudge,
Without a second or without a judge:
Truths would you teach, or save a sinking land?
All fear, none aid you, and few understand.

235 **Aurelius** Marcus Aurelius Antoninus, A.D. 121-180, Roman
emperor and philosopher 240 **Tully's** Cicero's 244 **Eugene**
Prince Eugene (1663-1736), eminent Austrian general 257
Marcellus opponent of Caesar, who settled at Mitylene

Painful pre-eminence! yourself to view
Above life's weakness, and its comforts too.
 Bring then these blessings to a strict account;
Make fair deductions; see to what they mount: 270
How much of other each is sure to cost;
How each for other oft is wholly lost;
How inconsistent greater goods with these;
How sometimes life is risked, and always ease:
Think, and if still the things thy envy call,
Say, wouldst thou be the man to whom they fall?
To sigh for ribands if thou art so silly,
Mark how they grace Lord Umbra, or Sir Billy:
Is yellow dirt the passion of thy life?
Look but on Gripus or on Gripus' wife.   280
If parts allure thee, think how Bacon shined,
The wisest, brightest, meanest of mankind:
Or ravished with the whistling of a name,
See Cromwell, damned to everlasting fame!
If all, united, thy ambition call,
From ancient story learn to scorn them all.
There, in the rich, the honored, famed, and great,
See the false scale of happiness complete!
In hearts of kings, or arms of queens who lay,
How happy! those to ruin, these betray.   290
Mark by what wretched steps their glory grows,
From dirt and sea weed as proud Venice rose;
In each how guilt and greatness equal ran,
And all that raised the hero, sunk the man:
Now Europe's laurels on their brows behold,
But stained with blood, or ill exchanged for gold:
Then see them broke with toils, or sunk in ease,
Or infamous for plundered provinces.
Oh wealth ill-fated! which no act of fame
E'er taught to shine, or sanctified from shame!   300
What greater bliss attends their close of life?
Some greedy minion, or imperious wife.
The trophied arches, storied halls invade
And haunt their slumbers in the pompous shade.
Alas! not dazzled with their noontide ray,
Compute the morn and evening to the day;
The whole amount of that enormous fame,
A tale that blends their glory with their shame!
 VII. Know then this truth (enough for man to know)
"Virtue alone is happiness below."   310
The only point where human bliss stands still,

And tastes the good without the fall to ill;
Where only merit constant pay receives,
Is blessed in what it takes, and what it gives;
The joy unequaled, if its end it gain,
And if it lose, attended with no pain:
Without satiety. though e'er so blessed,
And but more relished as the more distressed:
The broadest mirth unfeeling folly wears,
Less pleasing far than virtue's very tears: 320
Good, from each object, from each place acquired,
For ever exercised, yet never tired;
Never elated while one man's oppressed;
Never dejected while another's blessed;
And where no wants, no wishes can remain,
Since but to wish more virtue, is to gain.
    See the sole bliss Heaven could on all bestow!
Which who but feels can taste, but thinks can know:
Yet poor with fortune, and with learning blind,
The bad must miss; the good, untaught, will find;   330
Slave to no sect, who takes no private road,
But looks through Nature up to Nature's God;
Pursues that chain which links th' immense design,
Joins heaven and earth, and mortal and divine;
Sees, that no being any bliss can know,
But touches some above, and some below;
Learns, from this union of the rising whole,
The first, last purpose of the human soul;
And knows where faith, law, morals, all began,
All end, in love of God, and love of man.   340
For him alone, hope leads from goal to goal,
And opens still, and opens on his soul;
Till lengthened on to faith, and unconfined,
It pours the bliss that fills up all the mind.
He sees why Nature plants in man alone
Hope of known bliss, and faith in bliss unknown:
(Nature, whose dictates to no other kind
Are given in vain, but what they seek they find)
Wise is her present; she connects in this
His greatest virtue with his greatest bliss;   350
At once his own bright prospect to be blessed,
And strongest motive to assist the rest.
    Self-love thus pushed to social, to divine,
Gives thee to make thy neighbor's blessing thine.
Is this too little for the boundless heart?
Extend it, let thy enemies have part:

Grasp the whole worlds of reason, life, and sense,
In one close system of benevolence:
Happier as kinder, in whate'er degree,
And height of bliss but height of charity. 360
   God loves from whole to parts: but human soul
Must rise from individual to the whole.
Self-love but serves the virtuous mind to wake,
As the small pebble stirs the peaceful lake;
The center moved, a circle straight succeeds,
Another still, and still another spreads;
Friend, parent, neighbor, first it will embrace;
His country next; and next all human race;
Wide and more wide, th' o'erflowings of the mind
Take every creature in, of every kind; 370
Earth smiles around, with boundless bounty blest,
And heaven beholds its image in his breast.
   Come then, my friend! my genius! come along;
Oh master of the poet and the song!
And while the Muse now stoops, or now ascends,
To man's low passions, or their glorious ends,
Teach me, like thee, in various nature wise,
To fall with dignity, with temper rise;
Formed by thy converse, happily to steer
From grave to gay, from lively to severe; 380
Correct with spirit, eloquent with ease,
Intent to reason, or polite to please.
Oh! while along the stream of time thy name
Expanded flies, and gathers all its fame,
Say, shall my little bark attendant sail,
Pursue the triumph, and partake the gale?
When statesmen, heroes, kings, in dust repose,
Whose sons shall blush their fathers were thy foes,
Shall then this verse to future age pretend
Thou wert my guide, philosopher, and friend? 390
That urged by thee, I turned the tuneful art
From sounds to things, from fancy to the heart;
For wit's false mirror held up Nature's light;
Showed erring pride,—Whatever is, is right;
That reason, passion, answer one great aim;
That true self-love and social are the same;
That virtue only makes our bliss below;
And all our knowledge is,—Ourselves to know.

1733-1734

MORAL ESSAYS

Epistle II

TO A LADY

OF THE CHARACTERS OF WOMEN

NOTHING so true as what you once let fall,
"Most women have no characters at all."
Matter too soft a lasting mark to bear,
And best distinguished by black, brown, or fair.
   How many pictures of one nymph we view,
All how unlike each other, all how true!
Arcadia's Countess, here, in ermined pride,
Is, there, Pastora by a fountain side.
Here Fannia, leering on her own good man,
And there, a naked Leda with a swan.   10
Let then the fair one beautifully cry,
In Magdalen's loose hair and lifted eye,
Or dressed in smiles of sweet Cecilia shine,
With simpering angels, palms, and harps divine;
Whether the charmer sinner it, or saint it,
If folly grow romantic, I must paint it.
   Come, then, the colors and the ground prepare!
Dip in the rainbow, trick her off in air;
Choose a firm cloud before it fall, and in it
Catch, ere she change, the Cynthia of this minute.   20
   Rufa, whose eye quick-glancing o'er the park,
Attracts each light gay meteor of a spark,
Agrees as ill with Rufa studying Locke,
As Sappho's diamonds with her dirty smock;
Or Sappho at her toilet's greasy task,
With Sappho fragrant at an evening mask:
So morning insects, that in muck begun,
Shine, buzz, and fly-blow in the setting sun.
   How soft is Silia! fearful to offend;
The frail one's advocate, the weak one's friend: 30
To her, Calista proved her conduct nice;

To a Lady Martha Blount, Pope's intimate friend, especially in
the second half of his life 7-13 Arcadia's . . . Cecilia "attitudes
in which several ladies affected to be drawn, and sometimes
one lady in them all"—POPE 24 Sappho Lady Mary Wortley
Montagu, whose slovenliness was a matter of general comment

And good Simplicius asks of her advice.
Sudden, she storms! she raves! You tip the wink,
But spare your censure; Silia does not drink.
All eyes may see from what the change arose,
All eyes may see—a pimple on her nose.
  Papillia, wedded to her amorous spark,
Sighs for the shades—"How charming is a park!"
A park is purchased, but the fair he sees
All bathed in tears—"Oh odious, odious trees!"   40
  Ladies, like variegated tulips, show,
'Tis to their changes half their charms we owe;
Fine by defect, and delicately weak,
Their happy spots the nice admirer take.
'Twas thus Calypso once each heart alarmed,
Awed without virtue, without beauty charmed;
Her tongue bewitched as oddly as her eyes,
Less wit than mimic, more a wit than wise;
Strange graces still, and stranger flights she had,
Was just not ugly, and was just not mad;   50
Yet ne'er so sure our passion to create,
As when she touched the brink of all we hate.
  Narcissa's nature, tolerably mild,
To make a wash, would hardly stew a child;
Has even been proved to grant a lover's prayer,
And paid a tradesman once to make him stare;
Gave alms at Easter, in a Christian trim,
And made a widow happy, for a whim.
Why then declare good-nature is her scorn,
When 'tis by that alone she can be borne?   60
Why pique all mortals, yet affect a name?
A fool to pleasure, yet a slave to fame:
Now deep in Taylor and the Book of Martyrs,
Now drinking citron with his grace and Chartres:
Now conscience chills her, and now passion burns;
And atheism and religion take their turns;
A very heathen in the carnal part,
Yet still a sad, good Christian at her heart.
  See Sin in state, majestically drunk;
Proud as a peeress, prouder as a punk;   70
Chaste to her husband, frank to all beside,
A teeming mistress, but a barren bride.
What then? let blood and body bear the fault,
Her head's untouched, that noble seat of thought:

54 **a wash** lotion for the hair or skin 63 **Taylor** Jeremy Taylor
author of *Holy Living* and *Holy Dying*

Such this day's doctrine—in another fit
She sins with poets through pure love of wit.
What has not fired her bosom or her brain?
Caesar and Tall-boy, Charles and Charlemagne.
As Helluo, late dictator of the feast,
The nose of *hautgout* and the tip of taste,　　　　　80
Critiqued your wine, and analyzed your meat,
Yet on plain pudding deigned at home to eat;
So Philomedé, lecturing all mankind
On the soft passion, and the taste refined,
Th' address, the delicacy—stoops at once,
And makes her hearty meal upon a dunce.

　　Flavia's a wit, has too much sense to pray;
To toast our wants and wishes, is her way;
Nor asks of God, but of her stars, to give
The mighty blessing, "while we live, to live."　　90
Then all for death, that opiate of the soul!
Lucretia's dagger, Rosamonda's bowl.
Say, what can cause such impotence of mind?
A spark too fickle, or a spouse too kind.
Wise wretch! with pleasures too refined to please;
With too much spirit to be e'er at ease;
With too much quickness ever to be taught;
With too much thinking to have common thought:
You purchase pain with all that joy can give,
And die of nothing but a rage to live.　　　　　100
　　Turn then from wits; and look on Simo's mate,
No ass so meek, no ass so obstinate.
Or her, that owns her faults, but never mends,
Because she's honest, and the best of friends.
Or her, whose life the church and scandal share,
For ever in a passion, or a prayer.
Or her, who laughs at hell, but (like her grace)
Cries, "Ah! how charming if there's no such place!"
Or who in sweet vicissitude appears
Of mirth and opium, ratafie and tears,　　　　　110
The daily anodyne, and nightly draught,
To kill those foes to fair ones, time and thought.
Woman and fool are two hard things to hit;
For true no-meaning puzzles more than wit.

78 **Tall-boy** comic lover in Brome's comedy, *The Jovial Crew*
80 **hautgout** meat with a gamey taste　92 **Lucretia** Roman matron who stabbed herself after being raped by Tarquin　**Rosamonda** mistress of Henry II, forced to take poison by the jealous Queen　110 **ratafie** a kind of brandy

But what are these to great Atossa's mind?
Scarce once herself, by turns all womankind!
Who, with herself, or others, from her birth
Finds all her life one warfare upon earth:
Shines, in exposing knaves, and painting fools,
Yet is, whate'er she hates and ridicules.   120
No thought advances, but her eddy brain
Whisks it about, and down it goes again.
Full sixty years the world has been her trade,
The wisest fool much time has ever made.
From loveless youth to unrespected age,
No passion gratified except her rage.
So much the fury still outran the wit,
The pleasure missed her, and the scandal hit.
Who breaks with her, provokes revenge from hell,
But he's a bolder man who dares be well.   130
Her every turn with violence pursued,
No more a storm her hate than gratitude.
To that each passion turns, or soon or late;
Love, if it makes her yield, must make her hate:
Superiors? death! and equals? what a curse!
But an inferior not dependant? worse.
Offend her, and she knows not to forgive;
Oblige her, and she'll hate you while you live:
But die, and she'll adore you—Then the bust
And temple rise—then fall again to dust.   140
Last night, her lord was all that's good and great;
A knave this morning, and his will a cheat.
Strange! by the means defeated of the ends,
By spirit robbed of power, by warmth of friends,
By wealth of followers! without one distress
Sick of herself through very selfishness!
Atossa, cursed with every granted prayer,
Childless with all her children, wants an heir.
To heirs unknown descends th' unguarded store,
Or wanders, heaven-directed, to the poor.   150
    Pictures like these, dear Madam, to design,
Asks no firm hand, and no unerring line;
Some wandering touches, some reflected light,
Some flying stroke alone can hit 'em right:
For how should equal colors do the knack?
Chameleons who can paint in white and black?

115 **Atossa** probably Katherine Darnley, Duchess of Bucking-
hamshire, natural daughter of James II and half sister of the
Pretender

"Yet Chloe sure was formed without a spot"—
Nature in her then erred not, but forgot.
"With every pleasing, every prudent part,
Say, what can Chloe want?"—She wants a heart.   160
She speaks, behaves, and acts, just as she ought;
But never, never reached one generous thought.
Virtue she finds too painful an endeavor,
Content to dwell in decencies for ever.
So very reasonable, so unmoved,
As never yet to love, or to be loved.
She, while her lover pants upon her breast,
Can mark the figures on an Indian chest;
And when she sees her friend in deep despair,
Observes how much a chintz exceeds mohair.   17C
Forbid it Heaven, a favor or a debt
She e'er should cancel—but she may forget.
Safe is your secret still in Chloe's ear;
But none of Chloe's shall you ever hear.
Of all her dears she never slandered one,
But cares not if a thousand are undone.
Would Chloe know if you're alive or dead?
She bids her footman put it in her head.
Chloe is prudent—would you too be wise?
Then never break your heart when Chloe dies.   180
   One certain portrait may (I grant) be seen,
Which Heaven has varnished out, and made a **queen**:
The same for ever! and described by all
With truth and goodness, as with crown and ball.
Poets heap virtues, painters gems at will,
And show their zeal, and hide their want of skill.
'Tis well—but, artists! who can paint or write,
To draw the naked is your true delight.
That robe of quality so struts and swells,
None see what parts of nature it conceals: 190
Th' exactest traits of body or of mind,
We owe to models of an humble kind.
If Queensberry to strip there's no compelling,
'Tis from a handmaid we must take a Helen.
From peer or bishop 'tis no easy thing
To draw the man who loves his God, or king:
Alas! I copy (or my draught would fail)
From honest Mahomet, or plain Parson Hale.

193 **Queensberry** the Duchess of Queensberry, one of the most
beautiful women of the age 198 **Mahomet** Turkish servant of
George I **Parson Hale** Dr. Stephen Hales, curate of Teddington
and distinguished physiologist

But grant, in public men sometimes are shown,
A woman's seen in private life alone: 200
Our bolder talents in full light displayed;
Your virtues open fairest in the shade.
Bred to disguise, in public 'tis you hide;
There, none distinguish 'twixt your shame or pride,
Weakness or delicacy; all so nice,
That each may seem a virtue, or a vice.
   In men, we various ruling passions find;
In women, two almost divide the kind;
Those, only fixed, they first or last obey,
The love of pleasure, and the love of sway.   210
   That, Nature gives; and where the lesson taught
Is but to please, can pleasure seem a fault?
Experience, this; by man's oppression cursed,
They seek the second not to lose the first.
   Men, some to business, some to pleasure take;
But every woman is at heart a rake:
Men, some to quiet, some to public strife;
But every lady would be queen for life.
   Yet mark the fate of a whole sex of queens!
Power all their end, but beauty all the means: 220
In youth they conquer with so wild a rage,
As leaves them scarce a subject in their age:
For foreign glory, foreign joy, they roam;
No thought of peace or happiness at home.
But wisdom's triumph is well-timed retreat,
As hard a science to the fair as great!
Beauties, like tyrants, old and friendless grown,
Yet hate repose, and dread to be alone,
Worn out in public, weary every eye,
Nor leave one sigh behind them when they die.   230
   Pleasures the sex, as children birds, pursue,
Still out of reach, yet never out of view;
Sure, if they catch, to spoil the toy at most,
To covet flying, and regret when lost:
At last, to follies youth could scarce defend,
It grows their age's prudence to pretend;
Ashamed to own they gave delight before,
Reduced to feign it, when they give no more:
As hags hold sabbaths, less for joy than spite,
So these their merry, miserable night;   240
Still round and round the ghosts of beauty glide,
And haunt the places where their honor died.
   See how the world its veterans rewards!

A youth of frolics, an old age of cards;
Fair to no purpose, artful to no end,
Young without lovers, old without a friend;
A fop their passion, but their prize a sot,
Alive, ridiculous, and dead, forgot!
    Ah, friend! to dazzle let the vain design;
To raise the thought and touch the heart be thine!   250
That charm shall grow, while what fatigues the ring,
Flaunts and goes down, an unregarded thing:
So when the sun's broad beam has tired the sight,
All mild ascends the moon's more sober light,
Serene in virgin modesty she shines,
And unobserved the glaring orb declines.
    Oh! blessed with temper, whose unclouded ray
Can make tomorrow cheerful as today;
She, who can love a sister's charms, or hear
Sighs for a daughter with unwounded ear;   260
She, who ne'er answers till a husband cools,
Or, if she rules him, never shows she rules;
Charms by accepting, by submitting sways,
Yet has her humor most when she obeys;
Let fops or fortune fly which way they will,
Disdains all loss of tickets, or codille;
Spleen, vapors, or smallpox, above them all,
And mistress of herself, though China fall.
    And yet, believe me, good as well as ill,
Woman's at best a contradiction still.   270
Heaven, when it strives to polish all it can
Its last best work, but forms a softer man;
Picks from each sex, to make the favorite blessed,
Your love of pleasure, our desire of rest:
Blends, in exception to all general rules,
Your taste of follies, with our scorn of fools:
Reserve with frankness, art with truth allied,
Courage with softness, modesty with pride;
Fixed principles, with fancy ever new;
Shakes all together, and produces—you.   280
    Be this a woman's fame: with this unblessed,
Toasts live a scorn, and queens may die a jest.
This Phoebus promised (I forget the year)
When those blue eyes first opened on the sphere;
Ascendant Phoebus watched that hour with care,

251 the ring fashionable carriage-drive in Hyde Park, London
266 tickets lottery tickets codille signifying that an opponent
has won the hand in the card game of omber

Averted half your parents' simple prayer;
And gave you beauty, but denied the pelf
That buys your sex a tyrant o'er itself.
The generous god, who wit and gold refines,
And ripens spirits as he ripens mines,   290
Kept dross for duchesses, the world shall know it,
To you gave sense, good humor, and a poet.

1735

Epistle to Dr. Arbuthnot

ADVERTISEMENT

This paper is a sort of bill of complaint, begun many years since, and drawn up by snatches, as the several occasions offered. I had no thoughts of publishing it, till it pleased some persons of rank and fortune (the authors of *Verses to the Imitator of Horace,* and of an *Epistle to a Doctor of Divinity from a Nobleman at Hampton Court*) to attack, in a very extraordinary manner, not only my writings (of which, being public, the public is judge), but my person, morals, and family, whereof, to those who know me not, a truer information may be requisite. Being divided between the necessity to say something of myself, and my own laziness to undertake so awkward a task, I thought it the shortest way to put the last hand to this Epistle. If it have anything pleasing, it will be that by which I am most desirous to please, the truth and the sentiment; and if anything offensive, it will be only to those I am least sorry to offend, the vicious or the ungenerous.

Many will know their own pictures in it, there being not a circumstance but what is true; but I have, for the most part, spared their names, and they may escape being laughed at, if they please.

I would have some of them know, it was owing to the request of the learned and candid friend to whom it is inscribed, that I make not as free use of theirs as they have done of mine. However, I shall have this advantage, and honor, on my side, that whereas, by their proceeding, any abuse may be directed at any man, no injury can possibly be done by mine, since a nameless character can never be found out, but by its truth and likeness.—POPE

P. SHUT, shut the door, good John! fatigued, I said,
Tie up the knocker, say I'm sick, I'm dead.
The Dog Star rages! nay 'tis past a doubt,

1 **John** Pope's servant, John Serle

All Bedlam, or Parnassus, is let out:
Fire in each eye, and papers in each hand,
They rave, recite, and madden round the land.
　　What walls can guard me, or what shades can hide?
They pierce my thickets, through my grot they glide,
By land, by water, they renew the charge,
They stop the chariot, and they board the barge.　　10
No place is sacred, not the church is free,
Even Sunday shines no sabbath-day to me:
Then from the Mint walks forth the man of rhyme,
Happy! to catch me, just at dinner-time.
　　Is there a parson, much bemused in beer,
A maudlin poetess, a rhyming peer,
A clerk, foredoomed his father's soul to cross,
Who pens a stanza, when he should engross?
Is there, who, locked from ink and paper, scrawls
With desperate charcoal round his darkened walls?　　20
All fly to Twit'nam, and in humble strain
Apply to me, to keep them mad or vain.
Arthur, whose giddy son neglects the laws,
Imputes to me and my damned works the cause:
Poor Cornus sees his frantic wife elope,
And curses wit, and poetry, and Pope.
　　Friend to my life! (which did not you prolong,
The world had wanted many an idle song)
What drop or nostrum can this plague remove?
Or which must end me, a fool's wrath or love?　　30
A dire dilemma! either way I'm sped,
If foes, they write, if friends, they read me dead.
Seized and tied down to judge, how wretched I!
Who can't be silent, and who will not lie:
To laugh, were want of goodness and of grace,
And to be grave, exceeds all power of face.
I sit with sad civility, I read
With honest anguish, and an aching head;
And drop at last, but in unwilling ears,
This saving counsel, "Keep your piece nine years."　　40
　　"Nine years!" cries he, who, high in Drury Lane,
Lulled by soft zephyrs through the broken pane,
Rhymes ere he wakes, and prints before Term ends,

13 **Mint** a region in London exempt from legal process, there-
fore a resort for debtors and criminals 21 **Twit'nam** Twicken-
ham, where Pope lived 23 **Arthur** Arthur Moore, M.P. 43
Term when the courts were in session, a favorable time for
putting new books on the market

Obliged by hunger, and request of friends:
"The piece, you think, is incorrect? why, take it,
I'm all submission; what you'd have it, make it."
   Three things another's modest wishes bound,
My friendship, and a prologue, and ten pound.
   Pitholeon sends to me: "You know his Grace,
I want a patron; ask him for a place."   **50**
Pitholeon libelled me—"But here's a letter
Informs you, Sir, 'twas when he knew no better.
Dare you refuse him? Curll invites to dine,
He'll write a journal, or he'll turn divine."
Bless me! a packet. " 'Tis a stranger sues,
A virgin tragedy, an orphan Muse."
If I dislike it, "Furies, death and rage!"
If I approve, "Commend it to the stage."
There (thank my stars) my whole commission ends,
The players and I are, luckily, no friends.   **60**
Fired that the house reject him, " 'Sdeath! I'll print it,
And shame the fools—Your interest, Sir, with Lintot."
Lintot, dull rogue! will think your price too much:
"Not, Sir, if you revise it, and retouch."
All my demurs but double his attacks;
At last he whispers, "Do; and we go snacks."
Glad of a quarrel, straight I clap the door,
"Sir, let me see your works and you no more."
   'Tis sung, when Midas' ears began to spring,
(Midas, a sacred person and a king),   **70**
His very minister who spied them first,
(Some say his queen) was forced to speak, or burst.
And is not mine, my friend, a sorer case,
When every coxcomb perks them in my face?
   A. Good friend, forbear! you deal in dangerous **things.**
I'd never name queens, ministers, or kings;
Keep close to ears, and those let asses prick,
'Tis nothing—— *P.* Nothing? if they bite and kick?
Out with it, DUNCIAD! let the secret pass,
That secret to each fool, that he's an ass: **80**
The truth once told (and wherefore should we lie?)
The Queen of Midas slept, and so may I.
   You think this cruel? Take it for a rule,
No creature smarts so little as a fool.
Let peals of laughter, Codrus! round thee break,

53 **Curll** Edmund Curll, notorious publisher of libels, pornog·
raphy, and pirated books   62 **Lintot** Bernard Lintot, highly
successful publisher, who published many of Pope's works

Thou unconcerned canst hear the mighty crack:
Pit, box, and gallery in convulsions hurled,
Thou standst unshook amidst a bursting world.
Who shames a scribbler? break one cobweb through,
He spins the slight, self-pleasing thread anew: 90
Destroy his fib or sophistry, in vain,
The creature's at his dirty work again,
Throned in the center of his thin designs,
Proud of a vast extent of flimsy lines!
Whom have I hurt? has poet yet, or peer,
Lost the arched eyebrow, or Parnassian sneer?
And has not Colley still his lord, and whore?
His butchers Henley, his Freemasons Moore?
Does not one table Bavius still admit?
Still to one bishop Philips seem a wit?   100
Still Sappho—— A. Hold! for God's sake—you'll offend,
No names—be calm—learn prudence of a friend:
I too could write, and I am twice as tall;
But foes like these—— P. One flatterer's worse than all.
Of all mad creatures, if the learned are right,
It is the slaver kills, and not the bite.
A fool quite angry is quite innocent:
Alas! 'tis ten times worse when they repent.
    One dedicates in high heroic prose,
And ridicules beyond a hundred foes: 110
One from all Grub Street will my fame defend,
And, more abusive, calls himself my friend.
This prints my letters, that expects a bribe,
And others roar aloud, "Subscribe, subscribe."
    There are, who to my person pay their court:
I cough like Horace, and, though lean, am short,
Ammon's great son one shoulder had too high,
Such Ovid's nose, and "Sir! you have an eye"——
Go on, obliging creatures, make me see
All that disgraced my betters, met in me.   120
Say for my comfort, languishing in bed,
"Just so immortal Maro held his head":
And when I die, be sure you let me know
Great Homer died three thousand years ago.

97 Colley Cibber, who became the hero of *The Dunciad* **98
Henley** John Henley, eccentric preacher, who delivered a *Butch-
er's Lecture* at Newport Market **99 Bavius** Roman poetaster
satirized by Virgil **100 Philips** Ambrose Philips, Pope's early
rival as a writer of pastorals **101 Sappho** Lady Mary Wortley
Montagu **117 Ammon's great son** Alexander the Great **122 Maro**
Virgil

Why did I write? what sin to me unknown
Dipped me in ink, my parents', or my own?
As yet a child, nor yet a fool to fame,
I lisped in numbers, for the numbers came.
I left no calling for this idle trade,
No duty broke, no father disobeyed. 130
The Muse but served to ease some friend, not wife,
To help me through this long disease, my life,
To second, ARBUTHNOT! thy art and care,
And teach the being you preserved, to bear.
    But why then publish? Granville the polite,
And knowing Walsh, would tell me I could write;
Well-natured Garth inflamed with early praise;
And Congreve loved, and Swift endured my lays;
The courtly Talbot, Somers, Sheffield read,
Even mitred Rochester would nod the head, 140
And St. John's self (great Dryden's friend before)
With open arms received one poet more.
Happy my studies, when by these approved!
Happier their author, when by these beloved!
From these the world will judge of men and books,
Not from the Burnets, Oldmixons, and Cookes.
    Soft were my numbers; who could take offense
While pure description held the place of sense?
Like gentle Fanny's was my flowery theme,
A painted mistress, or a purling stream. 150
Yet then did Gildon draw his venal quill;
I wished the man a dinner, and sat still.
Yet then did Dennis rave in furious fret;
I never answered—I was not in debt.
If want provoked, or madness made them print,
I waged no war with Bedlam or the Mint.
    Did some more sober critic come abroad;
If wrong, I smiled; if right, I kissed the rod.
Pains, reading, study, are their just pretense,
And all they want is spirit, taste, and sense. 160
Commas and points they set exactly right,
And 'twere a sin to rob them of their mite.

135-139 **Granville . . . Sheffield** English authors, critics, and
amateurs of letters 140 **Rochester** Francis Atterbury, Bishop of
Rochester 141 **St. John's self** Henry St. John, Viscount Boling-
broke 146 **Burnets, Oldmixons, and Cookes** "Authors of secret
and scandalous history"—POPE 149 **Fanny's** Lord Hervey,
further treated below as Sporus 151 **Gildon** Charles Gildon,
mediocre poet, dramatist, and critic 153 **Dennis John Dennis,**
well-known critic, a long-time antagonist of Pope

Yet ne'er one sprig of laurel graced these ribalds,
From slashing Bentley down to piddling Tibbalds:
Each wight, who reads not, and but scans and spells,
Each word-catcher, that lives on syllables,
Even such small critics some regard may claim,
Preserved in Milton's or in Shakespeare's name.
Pretty! in amber to observe the forms
Of hairs, or straws, or dirt, or grubs, or worms!   170
The things, we know, are neither rich nor rare,
But wonder how the devil they got there.

    Were others angry: I excused them too;
Well might they rage, I gave them but their due.
A man's true merit 'tis not hard to find;
But each man's secret standard in his mind,
That casting-weight pride adds to emptiness,
This, who can gratify? for who can guess?
The bard whom pilfered Pastorals renown,
Who turns a Persian tale for half-a-crown,   180
Just writes to make his barrenness appear,
And strains, from hard-bound brains, eight lines a year;
He, who still wanting, though he lives on theft,
Steals much, spends little, yet has nothing left:
And he, who now to sense, now nonsense leaning,
Means not, but blunders round about a meaning:
And he, whose fustian's so sublimely bad,
It is not poetry, but prose run mad:
All these, my modest satire bade translate,
And owned that nine such poets made a Tate.   190
How did they fume, and stamp, and roar, and chafe!
And swear, not Addison himself was safe.

    Peace to all such! but were there one whose fires
True genius kindles, and fair fame inspires;
Blest with each talent and each art to please,
And born to write, converse, and live with ease:
Should such a man, too fond to rule alone,
Bear, like the Turk, no brother near the throne,
View him with scornful, yet with jealous eyes,
And hate for arts that caused himself to rise;   200
Damn with faint praise, assent with civil leer,
And, without sneering, teach the rest to sneer;
Willing to wound, and yet afraid to strike,

164 **Bentley** Richard Bentley, classical scholar **Tibbalds** Lewis
Theobald had taken Pope to task for the inadequacies of his
edition of Shakespeare. 190 **Tate** Nahum Tate (1652-1715), a
dreary versifier, made poet laureate in 1690 193-214 **The
"Atticus"** of this great portrait is Joseph Addison.

Just hint a fault, and hesitate dislike;
Alike reserved to blame, or to commend,
A timorous foe, and a suspicious friend;
Dreading even fools, by flatterers besieged,
And so obliging, that he ne'er obliged;
Like Cato, give his little senate laws,
And sit attentive to his own applause; 210
While wits and Templars every sentence raise,
And wonder with a foolish face of praise—
Who but must laugh, if such a man there be?
Who would not weep, if Atticus were he?
    What though my name stood rubric on the walls,
Or plastered posts, with claps, in capitals?
Or smoking forth, a hundred hawkers' load,
On wings of winds came flying all abroad?
I sought no homage from the race that write;
I kept, like Asian monarchs, from their sight: 220
Poems I heeded (now be-rhymed so long)
No more than thou, great George! a birthday song.
I ne'er with wits or witlings passed my days,
To spread about the itch of verse and praise;
Nor like a puppy, daggled through the town,
To fetch and carry sing-song up and down;
Nor at rehearsals sweat, and mouthed, and cried,
With handkerchief and orange at my side;
But sick of fops, and poetry, and prate,
To Bufo left the whole Castalian state. 230
    Proud as Apollo on his forkèd hill,
Sate full-blown Bufo, puffed by every quill;
Fed with soft dedication all day long,
Horace and he went hand in hand in song.
His library (where busts of poets dead
And a true Pindar stood without a head)
Received of wits an undistinguished race,
Who first his judgment asked, and then a place:
Much they extolled his pictures, much his seat,
And flattered every day, and some days eat: 240
Till grown more frugal in his riper days,
He paid some bards with port, and some with praise;
To some a dry rehearsal was assigned,
And others (harder still) he paid in kind.
Dryden alone (what wonder?) came not nigh,

215 **rubric** Titles of new books were commonly advertised in
red letters. 216 **claps** advertising posters 225 **daggled** trailed
about through wet and mire 230 **Bufo** probably Lord Halifax

Dryden alone escaped this judging eye:
But still the great have kindness in reserve,
He helped to bury whom he helped to starve.
    May some choice patron bless each grey goose quill!
May every Bavius have his Bufo still!   250
So when a statesman wants a day's defense,
Or envy holds a whole week's war with sense,
Or simple pride for flattery makes demands,
May dunce by dunce be whistled off my hands!
Blessed be the great! for those they take away,
And those they left me; for they left me GAY;
Left me to see neglected genius bloom,
Neglected die, and tell it on his tomb:
Of all thy blameless life the sole return
My verse, and QUEENSBERRY weeping o'er thy urn!   260
    Oh let me live my own, and die so too!
(To live and die is all I have to do:)
Maintain a poet's dignity and ease,
And see what friends, and read what books I please:
Above a patron, though I condescend
Sometimes to call a minister my friend.
I was not born for courts or great affairs:
I pay my debts, believe, and say my prayers;
Can sleep without a poem in my head,
Nor know, if Dennis be alive or dead.   270
    Why am I asked what next shall see the light?
Heavens! was I born for nothing but to write?
Has life no joys for me? or (to be grave)
Have I no friend to serve, no soul to save?
"I found him close with Swift"—"Indeed? no doubt,"
(Cries prating Balbus) "something will come out."
'Tis all in vain, deny it as I will.
"No, such a genius never can lie still";
And then for mine obligingly mistakes
The first lampoon Sir Will. or Bubo makes.   280
Poor guiltless I! and can I choose but smile,
When every coxcomb knows me by my style?
    Cursed be the verse, how well soe'er it flow,
That tends to make one worthy man my foe,
Give virtue scandal, innocence a fear,
Or from the soft-eyed virgin steal a tear!
But he who hurts a harmless neighbor's peace,
Insults fallen worth, or beauty in distress,
Who loves a lie, lame slander helps about,
Who writes a libel, or who copies out: 290

That fop, whose pride affects a patron's name,
Yet absent, wounds an author's honest fame:
Who can your merit selfishly approve,
And show the sense of it without the love;
Who has the vanity to call you friend,
Yet wants the honor, injured, to defend;
Who tells whate'er you think, whate'er you say,
And if he lie not, must at least betray:
Who to the dean, and silver bell can swear,
And sees at Canons what was never there;   300
Who reads, but with a lust to misapply,
Make satire a lampoon, and fiction, lie.
A lash like mine no honest man shall dread,
But all such babbling blockheads in his stead.
    Let Sporus tremble—— *A.* What? that thing of silk,
Sporus, that mere white curd of ass's milk?
Satire or sense, alas! can Sporus feel?
Who breaks a butterfly upon a wheel?
    P. Yet let me flap this bug with gilded wings,
This painted child of dirt, that stinks and stings;   310
Whose buzz the witty and the fair annoys,
Yet wit ne'er tastes, and beauty ne'er enjoys:
So well-bred spaniels civilly delight
In mumbling of the game they dare not bite.
Eternal smiles his emptiness betray,
As shallow streams run dimpling all the way.
Whether in florid impotence he speaks,
And, as the prompter breathes, the puppet squeaks;
Or at the ear of Eve, familiar toad,
Half froth, half venom, spits himself abroad,   320
In puns, or politics, or tales, or lies,
Or spite, or smut, or rhymes, or blasphemies.
His wit all see-saw, between that and this,
Now high, now low, now master up, now miss,
And he himself one vile antithesis.
Amphibious thing! that acting either part,
The trifling head, or the corrupted heart,
Fop at the toilet, flatterer at the board,
Now trips a lady, and now struts a lord.
Eve's tempter thus the Rabbins have expressed,   330

300 **Canons** elaborate estate of the Duke of Chandos, whose taste Pope had been charged with satirizing in his *Epistle to the Earl of Burlington* 305 **Sporus** Lord Hervey, author of the *Verses to the Imitator of Horace* named in Pope's "Advertisement" to this *Epistle*

A cherub's face, a reptile all the rest;
Beauty that shocks you, parts that none will trust,
Wit that can creep, and pride that licks the dust.
  Not fortune's worshiper, nor fashion's fool,
Not lucre's madman, nor ambition's tool,
Not proud, nor servile; be one poet's praise,
That, if he pleased, he pleased by manly ways:
That flattery, even to kings, he held a shame,
And thought a lie in verse or prose the same.
That not in fancy's maze he wandered long,   340
But stooped to truth, and moralized his song:
That not for fame, but virtue's better end,
He stood the furious foe, the timid friend,
The damning critic, half-approving wit,
The coxcomb hit, or fearing to be hit;
Laughed at the loss of friends he never had,
The dull, the proud, the wicked, and the mad;
The distant threats of vengeance on his head,
The blow unfelt, the tear he never shed;
The tale revived, the lie so oft o'erthrown,   350
The imputed trash, and dullness not his own;
The morals blackened when the writings 'scape,
The libelled person, and the pictured shape;
Abuse, on all he loved, or loved him, spread,
A friend in exile, or a father, dead;
The whisper, that to greatness still too near,
Perhaps, yet vibrates on his sovereign's ear—
Welcome for thee, fair Virtue! all the past:
For thee, fair Virtue! welcome even the last!
  A. But why insult the poor, affront the great?   360
  P. A knave's a knave, to me, in every state:
Alike my scorn, if he succeed or fail,
Sporus at court, or Japhet in a jail,
A hireling scribbler, or a hireling peer,
Knight of the post corrupt, or of the shire;
If on a pillory, or near a throne,
He gain his prince's ear, or lose his own.
  Yet soft by nature, more a dupe than wit,
Sappho can tell you how this man was bit:
This dreaded satirist Dennis will confess   370
Foe to his pride, but friend to his distress:
So humble, he has knocked at Tibbald's door,

341 **stooped** In falconry, the hawk is said to "stoop" to its prey.
363 **Japhet** Japhet Crook, a forger, whose punishment included
life imprisonment and the loss of his ears

Has drunk with Cibber, nay has rhymed for Moore.
Full ten years slandered, did he once reply?
Three thousand suns went down on Welsted's lie.
To please a mistress one aspersed his life;
He lashed him not, but let her be his wife:
Let Budgell charge low Grub Street on his quill,
And write whate'er he pleased, except his will;
Let the two Curlls of town and court, abuse   380
His father, mother, body, soul, and Muse.
Yet why? that father held it for a rule,
It was a sin to call our neighbor fool:
That harmless mother thought no wife a whore:
Hear this, and spare his family, James Moore!
Unspotted names, and memorable long!
If there be force in virtue, or in song.
   Of gentle blood (part shed in honor's cause,
While yet in Britain honor had applause)
Each parent sprung—— A. What fortune, pray?—— P.
   Their own,   390
And better got, than Bestia's from the throne.
Born to no pride, inheriting no strife,
Nor marrying discord in a noble wife,
Stranger to civil and religious rage,
The good man walked innoxious through his age.
No courts he saw, no suits would ever try,
Nor dared an oath, nor hazarded a lie.
Unlearned, he knew no schoolman's subtle art,
No language, but the language of the heart.
By nature honest, by experience wise,   400
Healthy by temperance, and by exercise;
His life, though long, to sickness passed unknown,
His death was instant, and without a groan.
O grant me thus to live, and thus to die!
Who sprung from kings shall know less joy than I.
  O friend! may each domestic bliss be thine!
Be no unpleasing melancholy mine:
Me, let the tender office long engage,
To rock the cradle of reposing age,

375 **Welsted's lie** Leonard Welsted, who had charged Pope with being himself responsible for the death of the lady lamented in Pope's *Elegy to the Memory of an Unfortunate Lady* 378 **Budgell** Eustace Budgell, man of letters, accused of forging the will of Matthew Tindal in his own favor 380 **the two Curlls** Edmund Curll and Lord Hervey 391 **Bestia's** L. Calpurnius Bestia, a venal Roman Consul

With lenient arts extend a mother's breath, 410
Make languor smile, and smooth the bed of death.
Explore the thought, explain the asking eye,
And keep awhile one parent from the sky!
On cares like these if length of days attend,
May Heaven, to bless those days, preserve my friend,
Preserve him social, cheerful, and serene,
And just as rich as when he served a queen.
    A. Whether that blessing be denied or given,
Thus far was right, the rest belongs to heaven.

1735

The Dunciad

The first three books of *The Dunciad* have chronicled the selection, by the Goddess of Dullness, of Colley Cibber to be King of the empire of Dullness; his coronation, together with the attendant ceremonial games; his sleep and dream-vision of the progress of Dullness in the past and present, and of its utter triumph in the future. In this fourth and concluding book, the triumph is consummated. Of the various devotees of the Goddess crowding around her throne on this occasion, the chief speakers represent school teachers; university dons; young gentlemen who pursue their education by means of a European tour; "virtuosi" who collect coins, butterflies, shells, and other curiosities; and the freethinkers who lose sight of God in the mazes of "high priori" philosophy. The aspiring youths are given to drink of a cup which causes oblivion of all knowledge and obligation, and the poem concludes with the Goddess uttering "a yawn of extraordinary virtue," which effects the total return of the civilized world to chaos and old night.

BOOK THE FOURTH

Yet, yet a moment, one dim ray of light
Indulge, dread chaos, and eternal night!
Of darkness visible so much be lent,
As half to show, half veil, the deep intent.
Ye powers! whose mysteries restored I sing,
To whom time bears me on his rapid wing,
Suspend a while your force inertly strong,

417 **served a queen** Dr. Arbuthnot had been physician to Queen Anne.

Then take at once the poet and the song.
 Now flamed the Dog Star's unpropitious ray,
Smote every brain, and withered every bay;   10
Sick was the sun, the owl forsook his bower,
The moon-struck prophet felt the madding hour:
Then rose the seed of chaos, and of night,
To blot out order, and extinguish light,
Of dull and venal a new world to mold,
And bring Saturnian days of lead and gold.
 She mounts the throne: her head a cloud concealed,
In broad effulgence all below revealed,
('Tis thus aspiring Dullness ever shines)
Soft on her lap her laureate son reclines.   20
 Beneath her footstool, science groans in chains,
And wit dreads exile, penalties, and pains.
There foamed rebellious logic, gagged and bound,
There, stripped, fair rhetoric languished on the ground;
His blunted arms by sophistry are borne,
And shameless Billingsgate her robes adorn.
Morality, by her false guardians drawn,
Chicane in furs, and casuistry in lawn,
Gasps, as they straiten at each end the cord,
And dies, when Dullness gives her Page the word. 30
Mad Máthesis alone was unconfined,
Too mad for mere material chains to bind,
Now to pure space lifts her ecstatic stare,
Now running round the circle finds it square.
But held in tenfold bonds the Muses lie,
Watched both by envy's and by flattery's eye:
There to her heart sad tragedy addressed
The dagger wont to pierce the tyrant's breast;
But sober history restrained her rage,
And promised vengeance on a barbarous age.   40
There sunk Thalia, nerveless, cold, and dead,
Had not her sister satire held her head;
Nor couldst thou, Chesterfield! a tear refuse,
Thou weptst, and with thee wept each gentle Muse.

---

26 **Billingsgate** foul or abusive language; the name derives from
a London fishmarket 30 **Page** Sir Francis Page (1661?-1741),
known as "the hanging judge" 31-34 **Mad Máthesis . . . square**
an allusion to mathematical theories of matter and space, and
to attempts to square the circle 41 **Thalia** muse of comedy 43
Chesterfield Lord Chesterfield, who opposed the Stage Licensing
Act in the House of Lords, 1737

When lo! a harlot form soft sliding by,
With mincing step, small voice, and languid eye:
Foreign her air, her robe's discordant pride
In patch-work fluttering, and her head aside:
By singing peers upheld on either hand,
She tripped and laughed, too pretty much to stand;   50
Cast on the prostrate Nine a scornful look,
Then thus in quaint recitativo spoke.
    "O Cara! Cara! silence all that train:
Joy to great chaos! let division reign:
Chromatic tortures soon shall drive them hence,
Break all their nerves, and fritter all their sense:
One trill shall harmonize joy, grief, and rage,
Wake the dull church, and lull the ranting stage;
To the same notes thy sons shall hum, or snore,
And all thy yawning daughters cry, 'Encore.'   60
Another Phoebus, thy own Phoebus, reigns,
Joys in my jigs, and dances in my chains.
But soon, ah soon, rebellion will commence,
If music meanly borrows aid from sense.
Strong in new arms, lo! Giant Handel stands,
Like bold Briareus, with a hundred hands;
To stir, to rouse, to shake the soul he comes,
And Jove's own thunders follow Mars's drums.
Arrest him, empress; or you sleep no more——"
She heard, and drove him to th' Hibernian shore.   70
    And now had fame's posterior trumpet blown,
And all the nations summoned to the throne.
The young, the old, who feel her inward sway,
One instinct seizes, and transports away.
None need a guide, by sure attraction led,
And strong impulsive gravity of head:
None want a place, for all their center found,
Hung to the goddess and cohered around.
Not closer, orb in orb, conglobed are seen
The buzzing bees about their dusky queen.   80
    The gathering number, as it moves along,
Involves a vast involuntary throng,
Who gently drawn, and struggling less and less,
Roll in her vortex, and her power confess.
Not those alone who passive own her laws,
But who, weak rebels, more advance her cause.
Whate'er of dunce in college or in town

45 harlot form Italian opera, then a frequent subject of ridicule
54 division technical term in music

Sneers at another, in toupee or gown;
Whate'er of mongrel no one class admits,
A wit with dunces, and a dunce with wits.   90
  Nor absent they, no members of her state,
Who pay her homage in her sons, the great;
Who, false to Phoebus, bow the knee to Baal;
Or impious, preach his word without a call.
Patrons, who sneak from living worth to dead,
Withhold the pension, and set up the head;
Or vest dull flattery in the sacred gown;
Or give from fool to fool the laurel crown.
And (last and worst) with all the cant of wit,
Without the soul, the Muse's hypocrite.   100
  There marched the bard and blockhead, side by side,
Who rhymed for hire, and patronized for pride.
Narcissus, praised with all a parson's power,
Looked a white lily sunk beneath a shower.
There moved Montalto with superior air;
His stretched-out arm displayed a volume fair;
Courtiers and patriots in two ranks divide,
Through both he passed, and bowed from side to side:
But as in graceful act, with awful eye
Composed he stood, bold Benson thrust him by: 110
On two unequal crutches propped he came,
Milton's on this, on that one Johnston's name.
The decent knight retired with sober rage,
Withdrew his hand, and closed the pompous page.
But (happy for him as the times went then)
Appeared Apollo's mayor and aldermen,
On whom three hundred gold-capped youths await,
To lug the ponderous volume off in state.
  When Dullness, smiling—"Thus revive the wits!
But murder first, and mince them all to bits;   120
As erst Medea (cruel, so to save!)
A new edition of old Æson gave;
Let standard authors, thus, like trophies borne,
Appear more glorious as more hacked and torn.
And you, my critics! in the chequered shade,
Admire new light through holes yourselves have made.

96 the head the bust commemorating a poet after his death
103 Narcissus Lord Hervey, notably pale in complexion **105
Montalto** Sir Thomas Hanmer, editor of Shakespeare **110 Ben-
son** William Benson, Whig politician, who set up a monument
to Milton in Westminster Abbey, and commissioned a bust of
Arthur Johnston, writer of Latin verse

"Leave not a foot of verse, a foot of stone,
A page, a grave, that they can call their own;
But spread, my sons, your glory thin or thick,
On passive paper, or on solid brick.   130
So by each bard an alderman shall sit,
A heavy lord shall hang at every wit,
And while on fame's triumphal car they ride,
Some slave of mine be pinioned to their side."
   Now crowds on crowds around the goddess press,
Each eager to present their first address.
Dunce scorning dunce beholds the next advance,
But fop shows fop superior complaisance.
When lo! a specter rose, whose index-hand
Held forth the virtue of the dreadful wand;   140
His beavered brow a birchen garland wears,
Dropping with infant's blood, and mother's tears.
O'er every vein a shuddering horror runs,
Eton and Winton shake through all their sons.
All flesh is humbled, Westminster's bold race
Shrink, and confess the genius of the place:
The pale boy-senator yet tingling stands,
And holds his breeches close with both his hands.
   Then thus: "Since man from beast by words is known,
Words are man's province, words we teach alone.   150
When reason doubtful, like the Samian letter,
Points him two ways, the narrower is the better.
Placed at the door of learning, youth to guide,
We never suffer it to stand too wide.
To ask, to guess, to know, as they commence,
As fancy opens the quick springs of sense,
We ply the memory, we load the brain,
Bind rebel wit, and double chain on chain;
Confine the thought, to exercise the breath;
And keep them in the pale of words till death.   160
Whate'er the talents, or howe'er designed,
We hang one jingling padlock on the mind:
A poet the first day he dips his quill;
And what the last? A very poet still.
Pity! the charm works only in our wall,

139 **a specter** ghost of Dr. Busby, famous headmaster of Westminster school. The following section, to l. 336, satirizes the classical education of the time. 151 **Samian letter** "Y", used by Pythagoras of Samos as emblem of the different roads to virtue and vice

Lost, lost too soon in yonder House or Hall.
There truant Wyndham every Muse gave o'er,
There Talbot sunk, and was a wit no more!
How sweet an Ovid, Murray was our boast!
How many Martials were in Pulteney lost!   170
Else sure some bard, to our eternal praise,
In twice ten thousand rhyming nights and days,
Had reached the work, the All that mortal can;
And South beheld that masterpiece of man."
  "Oh" (cried the goddess) "for some pedant reign!
Some gentle James, to bless the land again;
To stick the doctor's chair into the throne,
Give law to words, or war with words alone,
Senates and courts with Greek and Latin rule,
And turn the council to a grammar school!   180
For sure, if Dullness sees a grateful day,
'Tis in the shade of arbitrary sway.
Oh! if my sons may learn one earthly thing,
Teach but that one, sufficient for a king;
That which my priests, and mine alone, maintain,
Which as it dies, or lives, we fall, or reign:
May you, may Cam and Isis, preach it long!
'The Right Divine of kings to govern wrong.' "
  Prompt at the call, around the goddess roll
Broad hats, and hoods, and caps, a sable shoal: 190
Thick and more thick the black blockade extends,
A hundred head of Aristotle's friends.
Nor wert thou, Isis! wanting to the day,
Though Christ Church long kept prudishly away.
Each staunch polemic, stubborn as a rock,
Each fierce logician, still expelling Locke,
Came whip and spur, and dashed through thin and thick
On German Crousaz, and Dutch Burgersdyck.
As many quit the streams that murmuring fall
To lull the sons of Margaret and Clare Hall,   200

166 **House or Hall** the House of Commons, and Westminster
Hall   167-70 **Wyndham . . . Talbot . . . Murray . . . Pul-
teney** well-known statesmen; the two latter had also authored
Latin verses   174 **masterpiece** i.e., a verse epigram, which Dr.
South had said to be as difficult a literary performance as an
epic poem   176 **James** King James I   187 **Cam and Isis** Cam-
bridge and Oxford Universities   194 **Christ Church** a college at
Oxford   198 **Crousaz** Swiss philosopher **Burgersdyck** Dutch
philosopher   200 **Margaret** St. John's College, Cambridge,
established by Lady Margaret Beaufort   **Clare Hall** another
college at Cambridge

Where Bentley late tempestuous wont to sport
In troubled waters, but now sleeps in port.
Before them marched that awful Aristarch;
Ploughed was his front with many a deep remark:
His hat, which never vailed to human pride,
Walker with reverence took, and laid aside.
Low bowed the rest: he, kingly, did but nod;
So upright Quakers please both man and God.
"Mistress! dismiss that rabble from your throne:
Avaunt—— is Aristarchus yet unknown?   210
Thy mighty scholiast, whose unwearied pains
Made Horace dull, and humbled Milton's strains.
Turn what they will to verse, their toil is vain,
Critics like me shall make it prose again.
Roman and Greek grammarians! know your better:
Author of something yet more great than letter;
While towering o'er your alphabet, like Saul,
Stands our Digamma, and o'ertops them all.
'Tis true, on words is still our whole debate,
Disputes of *me* or *te*, of *aut* or *at*,   220
To sound or sink in *cano*, O or A,
Or give up Cicero to C or K.
Let Freind affect to speak as Terence spoke,
And Alsop never but like Horace joke:
For me, what Virgil, Pliny may deny,
Manilius or Solinus shall supply:
For Attic phrase in Plato let them seek,
I poach in Suidas for unlicensed Greek.
In ancient sense if any needs will deal,
Be sure I give them fragments, not a meal;   230
What Gellius or Stobaeus hashed before,
Or chewed by blind old scholiasts o'er and o'er.
The critic eye, that microscope of wit,
Sees hairs and pores, examines bit by bit:
How parts relate to parts, or they to whole,
The body's harmony, the beaming soul,

201 **Bentley** formidable Cambridge scholar and editor, and
lover of port wine 203 **Aristarch** a severe critic, derived from
Aristarchus, a second-century commentator on Homer 206
Walker Vice-master of Trinity College, of which Bentley was
Master 218 **Digamma** Bentley had discovered and restored this
letter in the Homeric poems. 223-24 **Freind . . . Alsop** Latin
scholars, opponents of Benley 226-31 **Manilius . . . Stobaeus**
All these were minor writers in Latin and Greek.

Are things which Kuster, Burman, Wasse shall see
When man's whole frame is obvious to a flea.
"Ah, think not, mistress! more true dullness lies
In folly's cap, than wisdom's grave disguise.   240
Like buoys, that never sink into the flood,
On learning's surface we but lie and nod.
Thine is the genuine head of many a house,
And much divinity without a νοῦς.
Nor could a Barrow work on every block,
Nor has one Atterbury spoiled the flock.
See! still thy own, the heavy Canon roll,
And metaphysic smokes involve the pole.
For thee we dim the eyes and stuff the head
With all such reading as was never read: 250
For thee explain a thing till all men doubt it,
And write about it, goddess, and about it:
So spins the silkworm small its slender store,
And labors till it clouds itself all o'er.
    "What though we let some better sort of fool
Thrid every science, run through every school?
Never by tumbler through the hoops was shown
Such skill in passing all, and touching none.
He may indeed (if sober all this time)
Plague with dispute, or persecute with rhyme.   260
We only furnish what he cannot use,
Or wed to what he must divorce, a Muse:
Full in the midst of Euclid dip at once,
And petrify a genius to a dunce;
Or set on metaphysic ground to prance,
Show all his paces, not a step advance.
With the same cement, ever sure to bind,
We bring to one dead level every mind.
Then take him to develop, if you can,
And hew the block off, and get out the man.   270
But wherefore waste I words? I see advance
Whore, pupil, and laced governor from France.
Walker! our hat——" nor more he deigned to say,
But, stern as Ajax' specter, strode away.
    In flowed at once a gay embroidered race,
And tittering pushed the pedants off the place:

237 **Kuster . . . Wasse** learned classical scholars 244 νοῦς
nous, meaning mind, intellect 245-46 **Barrow . . . Atterbury**
Isaac Barrow, Master of Trinity, and Francis Atterbury, Bishop
of Rochester and Dean of Westminster 247 **Canon** pun on
artillery and the name of an ecclesiastical office

Some would have spoken, but the voice was drowned
By the French horn, or by the opening hound.
The first came forwards, with as easy mien,
As if he saw St. James's and the queen.   280
When thus th' attendant orator begun,
"Receive, great empress! thy accomplished son:
Thine from the birth, and sacred from the rod,
A dauntless infant! never scared with God.
The sire saw, one by one, his virtues wake:
The mother begged the blessing of a rake.
Thou gav'st that ripeness, which so soon began,
And ceased so soon, he ne'er was boy, nor man.
Through school and college, thy kind cloud o'ercast,
Safe and unseen the young Æneas passed: 290
Thence bursting glorious, all at once let down,
Stunned with his giddy larum half the town.
Intrepid then, o'er seas and lands he flew:
Europe he saw, and Europe saw him too.
There all thy gifts and graces we display,
Thou, only thou, directing all our way!
To where the Seine, obsequious as she runs,
Pours at great Bourbon's feet her silken sons;
Or Tiber, now no longer Roman, rolls,
Vain of Italian arts, Italian souls: 300
To happy convents, bosomed deep in vines,
Where slumber abbots, purple as their wines:
To isles of fragrance, lily-silvered vales,
Diffusing languor in the panting gales:
To lands of singing, or of dancing slaves,
Love-whispering woods, and lute-resounding waves.
But chief her shrine where naked Venus keeps,
And Cupids ride the lion of the deeps;
Where, eased of fleets, the Adriatic main
Wafts the smooth eunuch and enamored swain.   310
Led by my hand, he sauntered Europe round,
And gathered every vice on Christian ground;
Saw every court, heard every king declare
His royal sense, of operas or the fair;
The stews and palace equally explored,
Intrigued with glory, and with spirit whored;
Tried all hors-d'œuvres, all liqueurs defined,
Judicious drank, and greatly-daring dined;
Dropped the dull lumber of the Latin store,

280 **St. James's** St. James's Palace, in London   308 **lion of the deeps** i.e., Venice

Spoiled his own language, and acquired no more;   320
All classic learning lost on classic ground;
And last turned air, the echo of a sound!
See now, half-cured, and perfectly well-bred,
With nothing but a solo in his head;
As much estate, and principle, and wit,
As Jansen, Fleetwood, Cibber shall think fit;
Stolen from a duel, followed by a nun,
And, if a borough choose him not, undone;
See, to my country happy I restore
This glorious youth, and add one Venus more.   330
Her too receive (for her my soul adores)
So may the sons of sons of sons of whores,
Prop thine, O empress! like each neighbor throne,
And make a long posterity thy own."
Pleased, she accepts the hero, and the dame
Wraps in her veil, and frees from sense of shame.
   Then looked, and saw a lazy, lolling sort,
Unseen at church, at senate, or at court,
Of ever-listless loiterers, that attend
No cause, no trust, no duty, and no friend.   340
Thee too, my Paridel! she marked thee there,
Stretched on the rack of a too-easy chair,
And heard thy everlasting yawn confess
The pains and penalties of idleness.
She pitied! but her pity only shed
Benigner influence on thy nodding head.
   But Annius, crafty seer, with ebon wand,
And well-dissembled emerald on his hand,
False as his gems, and cankered as his coins,
Came, crammed with capon, from where Pollio dines.
Soft, as the wily fox is seen to creep,   351
Where bask on sunny banks the simple sheep,
Walk round and round, now prying here, now there,
So he; but pious, whispered first his prayer.
   "Grant, gracious goddess! grant me still to cheat,
O may thy cloud still cover the deceit!
Thy choicer mists on this assembly shed,
But pour them thickest on the noble head.
So shall each youth, assisted by our eyes,
See other Caesars, other Homers rise;   360

326 **Jansen, Fleetwood, Cibber** all well-known for gambling, among other things; the last is Colley Cibber, actor, dramatist, and "hero" of *The Dunciad* 328 **And, if a borough** Members of Parliament were immune from arrest for debt.

Through twilight ages hunt th' Athenian fowl,
Which Chalcis gods, and mortals call an owl,
Now see an Attys, now a Cecrops clear,
Nay, Mahomet! the pigeon at thine ear;
Be rich in ancient brass, though not in gold,
And keep his lares, though his house be sold;
To headless Phoebe his fair bride postpone,
Honor a Syrian prince above his own;
Lord of an Otho, if I vouch it true;
Blest in one Niger, till he knows of two."   370
    Mummius o'erheard him; Mummius, fool-renowned,
Who like his Cheops stinks above the ground,
Fierce as a startled adder, swelled, and said,
Rattling an ancient sistrum at his head:
    "Speakst thou of Syrian princes? traitor base!
Mine, goddess! mine is all the hornèd race.
True, he had wit, to make their value rise;
From foolish Greeks to steal them, was as wise;
More glorious yet, from barbarous hands to keep,
When Sallee rovers chased him on the deep.   380
Then taught by Hermes, and divinely bold,
Down his own throat he risked the Grecian gold,
Received each demigod, with pious care,
Deep in his entrails—I revered them there,
I bought them, shrouded in that living shrine,
And, at their second birth, they issue mine."
    "Witness, great Ammon! by whose horns I swore,"
(Replied soft Annius) "this our paunch before
Still bears them, faithful; and that thus I eat,
Is to refund the medals with the meat.   390
To prove me, goddess! clear of all design,
Bid me with Pollio sup, as well as dine:
There all the learned shall at the labor stand,
And Douglas lend his soft, obstetric hand."

361 **Athenian fowl** the owl, stamped on Athenian coins 363
Attys ancient king of Lydia **Cecrops** legendary founder of
Athens 364 **pigeon** from which Mohammed was said to receive
divine messages 366 **lares** Roman household gods 369-70 **Otho
. . . Niger** referring to the rare coins of the reign of these two
Roman emperors 371 **Mummius**, etc. Pope ridicules contempo-
rary collectors of mummies and other curiosities. 372 **Cheops** a
mummified King of Egypt 374 **sistrum** Egyptian musical in-
strument 376 **hornèd race** the horns of Jupiter Ammon, rep-
resented on Macedonian medals; cf. line 387 380 **Sallee rovers**
Moorish pirates; derived from Sallee, a port in Morocco 394
Douglas James Douglas, celebrated obstetrician

The goddess smiling seemed to give consent;
So back to Pollio, hand in hand, they went.
  Then thick as locusts blackening all the ground,
A tribe, with weeds and shells fantastic crowned,
Each with some wondrous gift approached the power,
A nest, a toad, a fungus, or a flower.   400
But far the foremost, two, with earnest zeal,
And aspect ardent to the throne appeal.
  The first thus opened: "Hear thy suppliant's call,
Great queen, and common mother of us all!
Fair from its humble bed I reared this flower,
Suckled, and cheered, with air, and sun, and shower,
Soft on the paper ruff its leaves I spread,
Bright with the gilded button tipped its head;
Then throned in glass, and named it Caroline:
Each maid cried, Charming! and each youth, Divine!   410
Did Nature's pencil ever blend such rays,
Such varied light in one promiscuous blaze?
Now prostrate! dead! behold that Caroline:
No maid cries, Charming! and no youth, Divine!
And lo the wretch! whose vile, whose insect lust
Laid this gay daughter of the spring in dust.
Oh punish him, or to th' Elysian shades
Dismiss my soul, where no carnation fades!"
He ceased, and wept. With innocence of mien,
Th' accused stood forth, and thus addressed the queen.
  "Of all th' enameled race, whose silvery wing   421
Waves to the tepid zephyrs of the spring,
Or swims along the fluid atmosphere,
Once brightest shined this child of heat and air.
I saw, and started from its vernal bower,
The rising game, and chased from flower to flower.
It fled, I followed; now in hope, now pain;
It stopped, I stopped; it moved, I moved again.
At last it fixed, 'twas on what plant it pleased,
And where it fixed, the beauteous bird I seized: 430
Rose or carnation was below my care;
I meddle, goddess! only in my sphere.
I tell the naked fact without disguise,
And, to excuse it, need but show the prize;
Whose spoils this paper offers to your eye,
Fair even in death! this peerless butterfly."
  "My sons!" (she answered) "both have done your parts:

398 A tribe the "virtuosi," or collectors of curios and objects
of scientific interest

Live happy both, and long promote our arts.
But hear a mother, when she recommends
To your fraternal care our sleeping friends.   440
The common soul, of Heaven's more frugal make,
Serves but to keep fools pert, and knaves awake:
A drowsy watchman, that just gives a knock,
And breaks our rest, to tell us what's o'clock.
Yet by some object every brain is stirred;
The dull may waken to a humming bird;
The most recluse, discreetly opened, find
Congenial matter in the cockle-kind;
The mind, in metaphysics at a loss,
May wander in a wilderness of moss;   450
The head that turns at superlunar things,
Poised with a tail, may steer on Wilkins' wings.
    "O! would the sons of men once think their eyes
And reason given them but to study flies!
See Nature in some partial narrow shape,
And let the Author of the whole escape:
Learn but to trifle, or, who most observe,
To wonder at their Maker, not to serve!"
    "Be that my task" (replies a gloomy clerk,
Sworn foe to mystery, yet divinely dark;   460
Whose pious hope aspires to see the day
When moral evidence shall quite decay,
And damns implicit faith, and holy lies,
Prompt to impose, and fond to dogmatize:)
"Let others creep by timid steps, and slow,
On plain experience lay foundations low,
By common sense to common knowledge bred,
And last, to Nature's cause through Nature led.
All-seeing in thy mists, we want no guide,
Mother of arrogance, and source of pride!   470
We nobly take the high Priori Road,
And reason downward, till we doubt of God:
Make Nature still encroach upon His plan;
And shove Him off as far as e'er we can:
Thrust some mechanic cause into His place;
Or bind in matter, or diffuse in space.

452 **Wilkins'** John Wilkins, one of the founders of the Royal
Society, who speculated about the possibility of human flight
459 **clerk** i.e., "cleric," characterized here as a spokesman for the
freethinkers who were opposed both to revelation and empiri-
cism as evidences for God   471 **high Priori** for "a priori," applied
to reasoning from supposedly self-evident principles

Or, at one bound o'erleaping all His laws,
Make God man's image, man the final cause,
Find virtue local, all relation scorn,
See all in self, and but for self be born: 480
Of nought so certain as our reason still,
Of nought so doubtful as of soul and will.
Oh hide the God still more! and make us see
Such as Lucretius drew, a God like thee:
Wrapped up in self, a God without a thought,
Regardless of our merit or default.
Or that bright image to our fancy draw,
Which Theocles in raptured vision saw,
While through poetic scenes the genius roves,
Or wanders wild in academic groves;   490
That Nature our society adores,
Where Tindal dictates, and Silenus snores."
    Roused at his name, up rose the bousy sire,
And shook from out his pipe the seeds of fire;
Then snapped his box, and stroked his belly down,
Rosy and reverend, though without a gown.
Bland and familiar to the throne he came,
Led up the youth, and called the Goddess, Dame.
Then thus: "From priest-craft happily set free,
Lo! every finished son returns to thee: 500
First slave to words, then vassal to a name,
Then dupe to party; child and man the same;
Bounded by Nature, narrowed still by art,
A trifling head, and a contracted heart.
Thus bred, thus taught, how many have I seen,
Smiling on all, and smiled on by a queen?
Marked out for honors, honored for their birth,
To thee the most rebellious things on earth:
Now to thy gentle shadow all are shrunk,
All melted down, in pension, or in punk!   510
So K* so B** sneaked into the grave,
A monarch's half, and half a harlot's slave.
Poor W** nipped in folly's broadest bloom,
Who praises now? his chaplain on his tomb.
Then take them all, oh take them to thy breast!
Thy Magus, Goddess! shall perform the rest."

488 **Theocles** rhapsodic philosopher in Shaftesbury's dialogue,
The Moralists 492 **Tindal** Matthew Tindal, deistic philosopher
Silenus a satyr, addicted to wine 511-513 **K*** . . . **B*** . . .
W* It is not certain to whom Pope was alluding 516 **Magus**
magician

With that, a wizard old his cup extends;
Which whoso tastes, forgets his former friends,
Sire, ancestors, himself. One casts his eyes
Up to a star, and like Endymion dies: 520
A feather, shooting from another's head,
Extracts his brain; and principle is fled;
Lost is his God, his country, everything;
And nothing left but homage to a king!
The vulgar herd turn off to roll with hogs,
To run with horses, or to hunt with dogs;
But, sad example! never to escape
Their infamy, still keep the human shape.
But she, good Goddess, sent to every child
Firm impudence, or stupefaction mild;   530
And straight succeeded, leaving shame no room,
Cibberian forehead, or Cimmerian gloom.
    Kind self-conceit to some her glass applies,
Which no one looks in with another's eyes:
But as the flatterer or dependent paint,
Beholds himself a patriot, chief, or saint.
    On others Interest her gay livery flings,
Interest that waves on party-colored wings:
Turned to the sun, she casts a thousand dyes,
And, as she turns, the colors fall or rise.   540
    Others the siren sisters warble round,
And empty heads console with empty sound.
No more, alas! the voice of fame they hear,
The balm of Dullness trickling in their ear.
Great C**, H**, P**, R**, K*,
Why all your toils? your sons have learned to sing.
How quick ambition hastes to ridicule!
The sire is made a peer, the son a fool.
    On some, a priest succinct in amice white
Attends; all flesh is nothing in his sight!   550
Beeves, at his touch, at once to jelly turn,
And the huge boar is shrunk into an urn:
The board with specious miracles he loads,
Turns hares to larks, and pigeons into toads.
Another (for in all what one can shine?)
Explains the *sève* and *verdeur* of the vine.
What cannot copious sacrifice atone?

520 a star worn by Knights of the Garter or Knights of the Bath
521 a feather worn in their caps by Knights of the Garter 532
Cibberian from Colley Cibber **Cimmerian** dark, dismal 549-62
On some, etc. "the miracles of French cookery"—POPE 556
sève . . . verdeur terms signifying the qualities of wines

Thy truffles, Perigord! thy hams, Bayonne!
With French libation, and Italian strain,
Wash Bladen white, and expiate Hays's stain.   560
Knight lifts the head, for what are crowds undone,
To three essential partridges in one?
Gone every blush, and silent all reproach,
Contending princes mount them in their coach.
    Next, bidding all draw near on bended knees,
The queen confers her titles and degrees.
Her children first of more distinguished sort,
Who study Shakespeare at the Inns of Court,
Impale a glow worm, or *vertú* profess,
Shine in the dignity of F.R.S.   570
Some, deep Freemasons, join the silent race
Worthy to fill Pythagoras' place:
Some botanists, or florists at the least,
Or issue members of an annual feast.
Nor past the meanest unregarded, one
Rose a Gregorian, one a Gormogon.
The last, not least in honor or applause,
Isis and Cam made doctors of her laws.
    Then, blessing all, "Go, children of my care!
To practice now from theory repair.   580
All my commands are easy, short, and full:
My sons! be proud, be selfish, and be dull.
Guard my prerogative, assert my throne:
This nod confirms each privilege your own.
The cap and switch be sacred to his grace;
With staff and pumps the marquis lead the race;
From stage to stage the licensed earl may run,
Paired with his fellow-charioteer, the sun;
The learnèd baron butterflies design,
Or draw to silk Arachne's subtile line;   590
The judge to dance his brother sergeant call;
The senator at cricket urge the ball;
The bishop stow (pontific luxury!)
An hundred souls of turkeys in a pie;

560-61 **Bladen** . . . **Hays's** . . . **Knight** English gamesters who
had settled in Paris. Robert Knight had been cashier of the
South Sea Company 562 **three** . . . **partridges** i.e., two par-
tridges dissolved to make sauce for a third. As in the rest of this
passage, there is an ironic parallel with matters of religion. 568
Inns of Court student lawyers who prefer the study of Shake-
speare to that of the law 570 **F.R.S.** Fellow of the Royal Society
576 **Gregorian** . . . **Gormogon** societies founded in ridicule of
the Freemasons

The sturdy squire to Gallic masters stoop,
And drown his lands and manors in a soup.
Others import yet nobler arts from France,
Teach kings to fiddle, and make senates dance.
Perhaps more high some daring son may soar,
Proud to my list to add one monarch more;   600
And nobly conscious, princes are but things
Born for first ministers, as slaves for kings,
Tyrant supreme! shall three estates command,
And make one mighty Dunciad of the land!"
   More she had spoke, but yawned—All Nature nods:
What mortal can resist the yawn of gods?
Churches and chapels instantly it reached;
(St. James's first, for leaden Gilbert preached)
Then catched the schools; the hall scarce kept awake;
The convocation gaped, but could not speak: 610
Lost was the nation's sense, nor could be found,
While the long solemn unison went round:
Wide, and more wide, it spread o'er all the realm;
Even Palinurus nodded at the helm:
The vapor mild o'er each committee crept;
Unfinished treaties in each office slept;
And chiefless armies dozed out the campaign;
And navies yawned for orders on the main.
   O Muse! relate (for you can tell alone,
Wits have short memories, and dunces none),   620
Relate, who first, who last resigned to rest;
Whose heads she partly, whose completely blessed;
What charms could faction, what ambition lull,
The venal quiet, and entrance the dull;
Till drowned was sense, and shame, and right, and wrong—
O sing, and hush the nations with thy song!

     .   .   .   .   .

   In vain, in vain—the all-composing hour
Resistless falls: the Muse obeys the power.
She comes! she comes! the sable throne behold
Of night primeval, and of chaos old!   630
Before her, fancy's gilded clouds decay,
And all its varying rainbows die away.
Wit shoots in vain its momentary fires,

608 **Gilbert** Dr. John Gilbert, Dean of Exeter, later Archbishop
of York 614 **Palinurus** Aeneas' pilot, who fell into the sea when
asleep at the helm; the allusion is to Sir Robert Walpole, the
Prime Minister

The meteor drops, and in a flash expires.
As one by one, at dread Medea's strain,
The sickening stars fade off th' ethereal plain;
As Argus' eyes by Hermes' wand oppressed,
Closed one by one to everlasting rest;
Thus at her felt approach, and secret might,
Art after art goes out, and all is night.   640
See skulking truth to her old cavern fled,
Mountains of casuistry heaped o'er her head!
Philosophy, that leaned on Heaven before,
Shrinks to her second cause, and is no more.
Physic of metaphysic begs defense,
And metaphysic calls for aid on sense!
See mystery to mathematics fly!
In vain! they gaze, turn giddy, rave, and die.
Religion blushing veils her sacred fires,
And unawares morality expires.   650
For public flame, nor private, dares to shine;
Nor human spark is left, nor glimpse divine!
Lo! thy dread empire, Chaos! is restored;
Light dies before thy uncreating word:
Thy hand, great Anarch! lets the curtain fall;
And universal darkness buries all.

1742-1743

641 truth Democritus had said that truth lay at the bottom of
a deep well, until he drew her out.

BIBLIOGRAPHY

POPE'S OWN WRITINGS

Griffith, R. H., *Alexander Pope: A Bibliography*, 2 vols., Austin, Texas, 1922, 1927.

The Poems of Alexander Pope, The Twickenham Edition, 10 vols., London, 1939 ff. The standard edition.

The Correspondence of Alexander Pope, ed. George Sherburn, 5 vols., Oxford, 1956.

LIVES OF POPE

Johnson, Samuel, "Pope," *Lives of the English Poets*, ed. G. B. Hill, Oxford, 1905, Vol. III.

Sherburn, George, *The Early Career of Alexander Pope*, Oxford, 1934.

CRITICISM AND INTERPRETATION

Blanshard, Rufus A., *Discussions of Alexander Pope*, Boston, 1960.

Brooks, Cleanth, "The Case of Miss Arabella Fermor," *The Well Wrought Urn*, New York, 1947.

Brower, Reuben, *Alexander Pope: The Poetry of Allusion*, Oxford, 1959.

Clifford, James L., and Landa, Louis A., editors, *Pope and His Contemporaries*, Oxford, 1949.

Edwards, Thomas R., *The Dark Estate: A Reading of Pope*, Berkeley, 1963.

Jack, Ian, *Augustan Satire*, Oxford, 1952.

Lovejoy, A. O., *Essays in the History of Ideas*, Baltimore, 1948. Essays IV-VI.

Olson, Elder, "Rhetoric and the Appreciation of Pope," *Modern Philology*, XXXVII, 1939-1940, pp. 13-35.

Rogers, Robert W., *The Major Satires of Alexander Pope*, Urbana, 1955.

Root, Robert K., *The Poetical Career of Alexander Pope*, Princeton, 1938.

Tillotson, Geoffrey, *On the Poetry of Pope*, 2nd ed., Oxford, 1950.

Tillotson, Geoffrey, *Augustan Essays*, London, 1961.

Williams, Aubrey, *Pope's Dunciad*, Baton Rouge, 1955.

Wimsatt, William K., Jr., "Rhetoric and Poems: The Example of Pope," *The Verbal Icon*, New York, 1958.